The Dumb Patient

How to Avoid Death by Doctor

By: Taajah M. Phenezy

i

The one thing I would say to folks is RESEARCH, RESEARCH, RESEARCH the health information yourself and make sure that you **_have_** caring, compassionate and knowledge**_able_** folks in your **_corner_**. After the second, third, fourth, etc. opinions from exceptional neurologists in Chicago including the Head of Neurology, at a prominent Chicago University, they ALL misdiagnosed me leaving me in a wheelchair and almost DEAD. Much prayer and fasting led me to the TRUTH.

Linda Brocato

The Dumb Patient

How to Avoid Death by Doctor

* Names are used to tell the story and the use of these names does not imply their endorsement of this book.

* This book contains strong language, pictures and profanity as needed to tell the story.

The Dumb Patient is dedicated to my brave son, Khaale'ghee (KJ) Phenezy. Thanks for being brave enough to allow me to share your story with the world. Your suffering and pain will save many lives. I love you.

A special dedication goes to my Mom, Mary Phenezy and my Dad, Alton Anderson. Thanks for being there to support K. J. and me during this difficult time. You're truly appreciated.

Additional thanks and tribute to Dr. Boyd Haley, Dr. Dave Kennedy, Dr. Diane Meyers, Dr. Amber Denham, Dr. Melanie McKnight, Dr. Georgette Seveire, Attorney Robert Reeves, Freya Koss, Marie Flowers, Linda Brocato, Leo Cashman & Attorney Charlie Brown. All of you have played an important role in KJ's recovery. Thank you!

First Edition: February, 2013

Printed in the United States of America

ISBN-13: 978-0615776224

A blind man sees what we who claim sight cannot

Must death come before us all before pure vision
enlightens our soul?

Awaken we must

For slumber has been our true enemy

Taajah M. Phenezy

Table of Contents

Introduction

Life has a funny way of throwing you curve balls and challenges. Those who have survived a storm or two will always tell you that GOD doesn't give you anything that you can't handle. For example, when I was 14 it was discovered that I have a genius I.Q. This discovery happened in a psychiatric ward (maybe we'll discuss this in another book). Most people would say that all geniuses are crazy. I beg to differ. I think that we're merely misunderstood. Being a genius has been a curse and a blessing. Why, you ask? Well, I'm a beautiful woman. When people see my beauty, they often attempt to ignore my brains.

All my life I've been blessed with miracles. When I was a little girl (maybe 3 or 4 years old), I snuck into the attic of a neighbor's home that my mom and I were visiting in Detroit, Michigan. I was later found in the attic playing with two, extremely vicious Doberman pinschers. The owner of the dogs said that no-one had ever been able to approach the dogs before. They were so afraid that the dogs would attack me that my Mom was told to tell me to get up slowly. That didn't work. I jumped up and said, 'Bye-bye doggies.'

When I was 12 years old, I out-ran a serial rapist and murderer in my West side, Detroit neighborhood. He chased me up my street on Hartwell between Fenkell and Puritan. I ran as quickly as I could to my aunt and uncle's house (Aunt Jackie & Uncle Cleonard). They lived next door to my family. When Uncle Cleonard opened the door, the rapist turned down the side street and ran away. When we called the police, they said that this man fit the description of a rapist they were looking for. This rapist didn't want to lose his prey, so months later he came back to make me a victim. Somehow, I convinced him to just rape (and stalk) me. For months he returned to my family's home and used me as a pawn.

I told no-one about the rapes at the time due to fear that he would kill me and my brother. My little brother had seen this evil man so much that he thought the rapist was my friend. He was too young to know better. At that time I was only a child, and I thought that I had made a horrible decision when I begged him to keep me alive; perhaps I should have let him kill me. As I matured, my wounds and scars healed and I learned to love myself and life again. It was years before I could share this story. To this day, I still tear up when I talk about it.

After I turned 13, I decided I didn't want to be the pawn of this horrible man anymore, so I ran away from home and I chose to live out on the cruel streets of Detroit. With GOD's miracle, I survived a deep stabbing on my right side (I still have the scar). I didn't go to the hospital that night. I merely curled up in a corner of an alley and put dirty rags on the wound to stop the bleeding. I thought I would die that night. I prayed for death, but GOD has an interesting way of giving you miracles that you don't recognize as a miracle at the time.

As I look back over my life, I acknowledge that GOD has bestowed miracle upon miracle unto me. I don't believe that I'm special. I'm sure that if you took an honest look into your life, you too will find miracles. The question is: Are you willing to see those things as miracles or coincidences? Choose wisely.

Hey, many people will even tell you that everything happens for a reason. It's always difficult to believe positivity when you feel like you're deep in the middle of hell, but once you make it out of darkness and regroup; you come to realize that those who wanted you to stay positive were actually right. The only thing left to do now is to figure out 'the reason' why 'it' happened.

Let me formally introduce myself. I am Taajah; the author of this book. In the business world, I've always used T. M. Phenezy so people didn't know that I was a woman until they met me. Trust me, in a male dominated, business world, this strategy got me into many doors. Over the last few years, I've learned some valuable lessons through trial and error. These trials almost cost the life of my son; my only child.

I was born and raised in Detroit, Michigan but at the

age of 14, I moved to a small town called New Roads, Louisiana to finish high school. From there, I joined the United States Marine Corps in 1987.

On September 16, 1993, on a naval base in Yokosuka Japan, I gave birth to an extremely healthy son, Khaale'ghee Jamil (now nicknamed KJ). He was born with a full head of hair and his big brown eyes were wide open. KJ came into this world at 8lbs, 7 oz. and 24 inches long. KJ was born in Japan because at that time, I was stationed there as a Sergeant (Sgt.) in the Marine Corps. KJ was so beautiful and just like the birth of a child to any family, he changed my life forever.

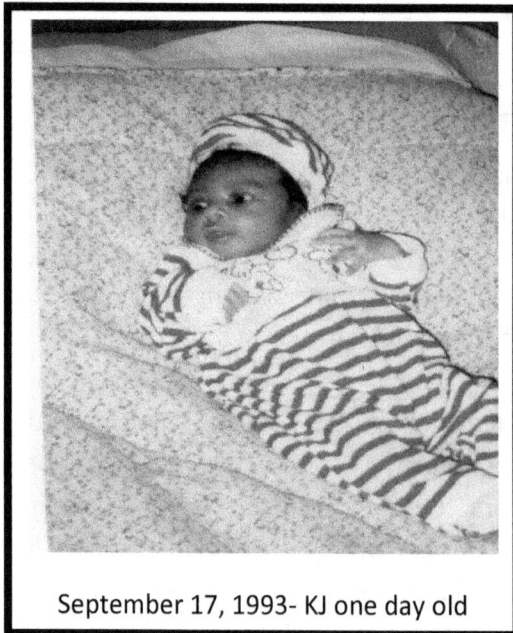

September 17, 1993- KJ one day old

In early 1994, I was transferred to Camp Pendleton, California. There we met a wonderful family, (The Sindens). Jim Sinden (a Marine) had a lovely wife, Margaret, and she was a certified home day care provider on base. Margaret and Jim have 3 beautiful daughters, Jennifer, Ashlee & Brittany. Margaret provided day care for KJ, but she and her family was more than daycare. They were family. I learned a lot from their family. All of them loved KJ so much. They're also witnesses to the wonderful health that KJ was in. Life was great!

Let's fast forward to when KJ was the age of 15. For his 15th birthday in September 2008, KJ was still the epitome of great health before he developed life threatening medical problems from a controversial situation shortly after his 15th birthday. I had to quickly teach KJ to pretend that he had cotton balls in his ears so that he could drown out the negativity spewed from the mouths of his doctors. KJ learned that although things were bad 'right now', doctors didn't know GOD's plan.

In March of 2009, experts told me that my beloved son would spend the rest of his life in a wheelchair. The experts also told me that because he got ill, so quickly, he would never have a normal life expectancy. KJ would have a very, very short life. They never said a specific date, but I don't think that they expected him to live another year. These 'experts' were even kind enough to initiate this conversation in front of KJ. Yes, I demanded that we move the conversation to the hospital hall.

After his doctors were kind enough to tell us that KJ would soon die in a wheelchair, we didn't burst out in tears. Of course, KJ had worry and concern written on his face. As for me, I had learned to mask any concerns because I knew KJ would respond to my emotions. For a short time, I didn't know what encouraging words I could say to my son. It was just the two of us. KJ's father (another U.S. Marine) was barely in his life. During this time, his father wasn't in his life at all, so I had practically been the only parent. KJ and I were truly close and he respected and trusted me.

I knew that GOD was putting KJ's life in my tiny hands. Trust me, I was petrified; but I knew that although my hands were tiny, they were also strong. Ever since my son got ill, I had been telling KJ that everything was going to be ok. How many times could I say these words before my son wouldn't believe me anymore? KJ was just a child. I was asking him to be stronger than most children and adults could ever imagine being. At such a young age, how could KJ have the faith in GOD that I had? Even as an adult, how could I keep my own faith from being shattered?

Sadly, KJ and I had never been regular church goers. We would visit a friend's church once a month or when someone invited us, but we didn't have a church 'home' of our own. Yes, I taught KJ right from wrong, but I had never really taught him the Word of GOD! I couldn't teach what I barely knew.

That's when I said it. I was driving KJ home from his doctor's appointment and I just blurted it out. I said, 'KJ, Mommy promises you that you will not spend the rest of your life in a wheel chair!' I said it and I couldn't take it back. I was bold. I was believable. I was horrified, but I had no choice but to execute a plan. Sadly, at that time I had no plan. I was accustomed to writing business plans for my clients, but to have to write a plan to save my son's life, that was unchartered territory for me. No college can prepare you for this.

Believe me when I tell you that there's nothing more painful than watching your child suffer immensely from a painful disease. Every day, many parents, friends and loved ones have to battle the bureaucratic hypocrisy of hospitals and healthcare. Many doctors and administrators have questioned my attitude. They constantly insulted my intelligence. Above all, doctors underestimated GOD's will as well as KJ's will to live. I was disappointed to see that most doctors were more into the words that were in their medical journals than they were into the practical application of what they had learned.

The number of deaths due to malpractice will never be reported accurately. I believe that hospitals and doctors have a financial incentive to link suspicious deaths to natural causes. If there is any doubt, the benefit usually goes to the doctor or hospital.

The **DUMB PATIENT** ... How to Avoid Death by Doctor is a guide for those who need to learn how to advocate for themselves or their loved ones. Walk in my shoes as I share my trans-formative journey with my son, KJ, and his healthcare. Grab a tissue for your tears and a pen to take notes in the back of this guide. Learn from my mistakes and rejoice from my triumphs.

Chapter 1

KJ's Story

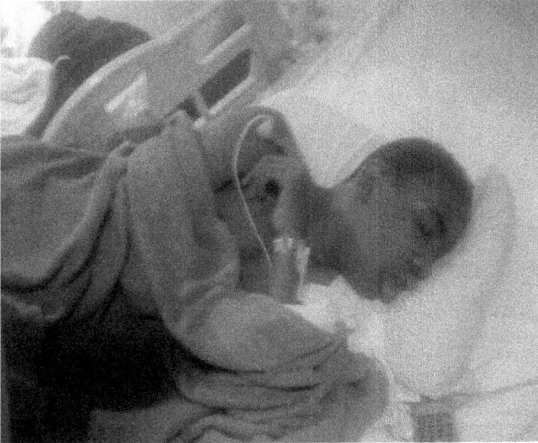

KJ, Children's Hospital San Diego, December 2008

I recently asked my son, KJ, if he has ever regretted leaving our beautiful home in California. He looked at me as if I was crazy and emphatically said, 'No. I would be dead if we hadn't!'

As a strong woman, I try not to cry very often, but I did cry that night. I tend to cry when I'm alone. Sometimes it's in the shower and sometimes I do so very quietly in bed. I've learned to comfort myself when I'm hurting because it hurts more to want someone to comfort you and no one is there, willing or able.

1

Dealing with my son's health has been a struggle, but his response to the California question lets me know that these struggles are worth it to him. It's surely worth it to me. After KJ got sick, he had to leave behind his home, friends and culture. He had to leave behind everything that he knew and loved. One of the most difficult days for KJ was when he had to give away his two dogs. They were his babies and there was no way that we could take them with us. KJ fed his dogs, slept with them, played video games with them and cleaned their poop. Like many parents, he often had to break up their 'sibling', doggie fights. I must reiterate that the dogs, Bruce and Brody were KJ's children. They were his responsibility.

Bruce and Brody were huge boxers so it wasn't easy to find a good home for them. KJ still has pictures of them in his phone. We often reminisce and share stories and pictures about Bruce and Brody.

Brody and Bruce as babies relaxing in the theater room.

I know you are wondering why a mother would have to uproot her child in order to find medical care out of state. I had no choice! KJ was literally dying and wilting away before the eyes of his friends and me. The medical care being provided by his doctors in California was not working. It was pure science with no art!

You must understand that my maternal instinct kicked in immediately. I knew what was wrong with KJ. Yes...I KNEW! I shared KJ's story many, many times to numerous California doctors. I always presented strong, logical, anecdotal (yet controversial) evidence.

I find it alarming that it is well known that when a laymen patient or his advocate often provides any evidence to a doctor that contradicts what doctors believe or have been taught, this evidence is chalked up to be coincidence or even unrealistic. When doctors provide 'evidence', (even if it's contrary to what's being seen) then their beliefs are considered medicine. Wow, that's sad.

Some doctors even thought that I was a tad bit crazy. I never denied being crazy. I like to say that I'm a controlled crazy. Heck, I am a U. S. Marine. However, being crazy is still a far fetch from being stupid.

Ultimately, I had done the research and acquired the knowledge, even still my maternal instinct, book sense, common sense and high intelligence didn't matter to any of these doctors. I looked like a young, African American Mom and they attempted to treat and

3

stereotype me as if I was ignorant and uneducated.

My 'maternal diagnosis' and beliefs were irrelevant. What I was presenting and proving to them was not taught in medical schools. My theory wasn't in their precious medical journals and it surely wasn't water cooler conversation. Thus, these closed minded doctors refused to listen to me. A few of them even yelled at me. Believe it or not, someone (anonymously) called child protective service on me. Of course, this call never turned into a case. What a joke!

Most of KJ's doctors refused to conduct any research of their own to determine if there was any merit to my argument. I was constantly labeled as unreasonable, overly aggressive, and irritating. God only knows what else was said behind my back.

Ok. I know that inquiring minds are trying to figure out what in the world happened to KJ. Let me take a little time to satisfy your humophotosngous curiosity. Remember, what you're about to read is merely the beginning and a small part of *KJ's Story*. My son had to be my OJT (on the job training) to becoming a **SMART PATIENT** and his patient advocate. I want you to learn from my experience and his suffering so that you and/or your loved ones have a fair chance of survival when dealing with our brutal healthcare system. Consider this guide to be your personal healthcare system, survival kit. Welcome to KJ's Story!

On September 16, 2008, KJ turned 15 years young.

4

He's my only child. Our home sat on a hill overlooking beautiful city lights in a small San Diego County, city. Our property was on three quarters of an acre and was full of beautiful flowers, fruits, palm trees with a lovely swimming pool and hot tub that we didn't properly maintain because it was never used. Springtime blooming from the windows of our home was a beautiful sight to see. If you wanted to get a glimpse of the city, all you had to do was go upstairs to our rooftop deck. Nights were especially pleasing.

KJ enjoyed spending time in 'his' theater room where he primarily played Xbox 360 and watched movies with his friends and dogs. One of his very best friends, Justin, would come over often. KJ loved playing basketball, movie nights with friends and trips to the mall. He enjoyed a normal, teenage life. KJ was (and still is) an extremely smart, happy, loving young man who besides the teenaged diarrhea mouth from time to time, KJ stayed out of trouble.

When KJ turned 15, he was very healthy. He had been healthy throughout his childhood. He and I had recently found out that he had flat feet (they're huge too), but other than that, there were no other health issues. He had always passed his sports physicals with flying colors. Growing up, he had never even had the flu, yet alone a flu shot. KJ was so healthy that he hadn't required any antibiotics since he was a baby with an ear infection. Neither one of us can even remember him ever taking Tylenol for a headache. I'm pretty sure that he didn't because, heck, at that time he couldn't even swallow pills. As one of the star players on his basketball team, KJ often played an entire game without resting. He was the epitome of health.

After his 15th birthday, KJ had decided that he was finally ready to overcome his fears of the dentist. Vanity is an interesting thing. KJ wanted and needed to get the Invisiline braces for his teeth, so he had to go to the dentist. On October 8, 2008, I took him to a local chain dentist in our city. They placed two amalgams (a.k.a. silver fillings) in his mouth. One was placed in his right upper molar and one in his right lower molar. 3 days later, KJ became ill with a fever of 102 - 102.9. His high fever lasted for 3 days.

This may sound crazy, but to me, it was actually kind of cute that KJ had a fever. Why? KJ finally had the flu for the first time in his life. No biggie. It's just the flu, right? He had most of the signs for the flu. His fever was accompanied by the expected chills and sweat. Except for the lack of mucus, it appeared as though KJ had a bad cold or flu. Now, just like every mommy, I figured that I would just baby my baby and this 'flu' would be over in a few days. I gave him over the counter Theraflu and we stayed home for three days so he could recuperate. Sounds like a typical flu, right? Wrong!

KJ's fever turned out to be a warning sign that something very drastic was happening to his body. A few days after his fever broke; KJ woke up with a swollen lip on his right side of his face. This unusual swelling dissipated after a couple of hours with no treatment from me. I actually thought that one of his dogs (Brody) had hit him in the face with his tail while KJ was sleeping. That was logical thinking, wouldn't you agree?

The next day KJ awakened with a swollen jaw on the right side of his face. The day next day, it was his eyelid... Ironically, the swelling began on the right side of his face where the new fillings were 'coincidentally' located.

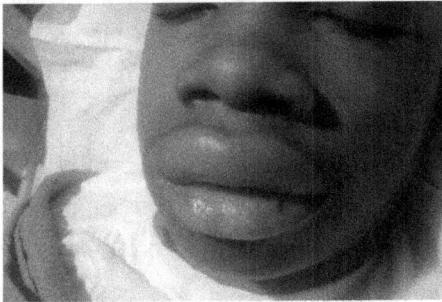

KJ, December 2008. Both lips and face swollen.

On day 2 of this strange swelling cycle, I believed that I recognized the correlation between the amalgam fillings and KJ's sudden onset of symptoms. Going to the dentist was the only thing we had done differently and since then KJ had been sick. Thus, I took KJ to see his primary care doctor to discuss the fillings.

Of course, when I asked his doctor about whether or

not there could be a relationship between the flu, swellings and the fillings, my concerns were quickly dismissed. Well, I was told that 'silver fillings' are controversial, but they don't make people sick! It takes a lot to confuse me, but this doctor managed to accomplish this great feat! Amalgams are controversial? What? I wasn't aware of any controversy. Better yet, why wasn't I aware of the controversy? At that time, I merely thought that KJ may have had an allergic reaction to the 'silver' in the amalgams. These fillings are silver, aren't they?

Anyway, it was obvious from the Doctor's remarks as to what side of the controversy he stood on, so there was no sense in me wasting my time asking him what he meant. KJ and I left the doctor's office with no explanation at all for the swellings on his face. We went straight home and I immediately began researching the 'controversy'. I know you're anxious, but I promise that I'll tell you what I learned about these dreadful fillings a little bit later.

KJ's symptoms continued to escalate. Rashes, tremors, burning of the throat and chest, anemia, lack of energy, metal taste in mouth, swellings, and more. Tests for acid reflux were normal and there were never any justifications or explanations as to why these things were happening to him.

By December 13, 2008, KJ was so ill that I demanded that his primary care doctor immediately have him admitted to the children's hospital in San Diego.

Upon admission, KJ received 2 blood transfusions and numerous lab tests. He was so sick! I'm a mom and I'm human, so it devastated my heart to see my son in so much pain. To make matters worse; the doctors had no idea what was wrong with him.

Every doctor and every specialist had a different theory. A few doctors even thought that he had lymphoma due to all the swollen lymph nodes in numerous places all over KJ's body. It was chaotic. For every theory there was a lab test, and a completely different 'possible diagnosis'. KJ was a pin cushion.

The two photos below were taken December 2008 and are indicative of swollen lymph nodes on his neck and underarm.

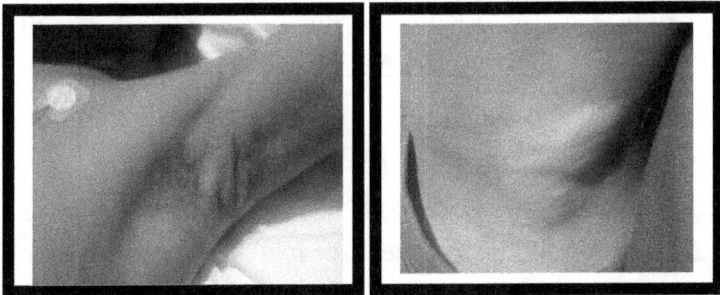

I'm not a weak woman by anyone's standards. Nor would I be considered ignorant by most. So, I realized that I had to actively participate in KJ's recovery. By December 2008, I had engaged in basic research of these amalgams and found that Amalgams are made of an alloy of mercury and other metals. They weren't really silver. Amalgams were nicknamed 'silver' fillings because of their silver color.

Amalgams were created by the Crawcour brothers in 1833. They were entrepreneurs, not dentists or doctors. The American Society of Dental Surgeons was the first dental association and they denounced the use of Amalgams. However, many dentists defied the association because this alloy was cheaper and easier than using gold. In 1859, the American Dental Association (ADA) was founded. Since its inception, the ADA has defended the use of Amalgams.

I also found that there is documented and admitted evidence by the ADA that a small amount of mercury leaks from the amalgam alloy and this leaking mercury enters the bloodstream. It turns out that the mercury in the fillings was never inert as most people had been led to believe. This lie had been told for over 100 years before anyone in support of these mercury fillings would begin to acknowledge the mercury leakage.

I desperately begged and begged Rady's Children's Hospital of San Diego to test for mercury poisoning due to the mercury fillings. Those who advocate against the fillings call it chronic low dose mercury poisoning. I pleaded my case and finally they tested KJ's blood for mercury poisoning. Thank GOD! Let's get these results and get him the needed treatment for mercury poisoning and go home. When the mercury test results came in, they showed that KJ **DID NOT** have an elevated mercury level. **NO MERCURY POISONING?**

Wow!? 'Are you sure?' I questioned the doctors. What I was unaware of (at the time) was that a blood test is one of the least effective ways to test for low dose, chronic mercury poisoning. At that time, I was an extremely *DUMB PATIENT!*

The doctors of Rady's Children's Hospital of San Diego used the mercury lab result to dismiss all of my concerns regarding the fillings and mercury poisoning. In a nice and political kind of way, they pretty much told me to get over it and move on. They proudly noted that the blood test proved that I was wrong. I wanted my son to get better, so what's a mom to do? I began to move on in my questioning. I asked no additional questions about mercury, mercury poisoning or amalgams.

Eventually KJ was diagnosed with lupus in December 08. His diagnosis escalated to Stage V, lupus nephritis (a kidney disease) in January 09. By March 9, 2009, KJ was in a wheel chair, diagnosed with peripheral neuropathy (nerve damage) in his lower extremities. Yep, this 'nerve' damage put my once active son was partially paralyzed in a wheelchair. His symptoms continued to quickly worsen even though KJ was on the proper medications (per doctors).

Throughout this dreadful process I was still quietly and diligently researching amalgams, lupus, lupus nephritis and mercury poisoning. Eventually, I was finally able to dig deeper than the shallow surface of information. As I mom, I wanted what was best for KJ, so I looked at research and information that discussed

11

both sides of the coin. I read the reports and research of those who said that these mercury fillings are safe and I also read the reports of those who said that these mercury fillings are dangerous. I was disgusted. What I found shocked, amazed, angered and saddened me. I quickly learned that up to this point, my research on amalgams and mercury poisoning had only scratched the surface.

These mercury fillings (a.k.a. amalgams and silver fillings) were already banned in several other countries and Canada had already placed strict restrictions on its use. Since its use in the 1800's the U.S. had never required the manufacturers to prove its safety.

In 1882, Dr. Eugene S. Talbot, M.D., D.D.S. warned the American Dental Association (ADA) about the safety of these fillings. Dr. Talbot told them that the fillings leaked mercury. He wrote about the danger of Amalgams in the Ohio State Journal of Dental Science, 1882 (the Pdf can be found at **TheDUMBPATIENT.COM**). Dr. Talbot's pleas of concern with his peers were ignored and many dentists continued to use the amalgams.

When The Food & Drug Administration (FDA) was formed (1930), amalgams were simply grandfathered in. Since mercury fillings (amalgams) preceded the FDA, amalgam distributors didn't have to prove its safety. In my extensive research, I also found that some people lose the ability to excrete the mercury from their body. When these people can't excrete the mercury, it gets stored in their tissues, causing more harm. Research shows that boys have a harder time excreting the mercury than girls.

Many people don't understand what all the big deal is regarding mercury. Mercury can even be found in many immunizations via a preservative called Thimerosol. Stop for a moment and imagine what your thought process would be if I told you that amalgams were approximately 50% lead in weight! You and every person you know would be totally outraged!

The Centers for Disease Control & Prevention (CDC), The National Institutes of Health (NIH), World Health Organization (WHO) and every researcher whom I've spoken with all agree that mercury is far more toxic than lead. I could provide numerous tables, links and quotes for you to review, but I don't want to be an enabler. I need you to seek out this information yourself. This is so much about common sense that we shouldn't even have to discuss it.

Mercury (also known as quicksilver) is far more toxic than lead. The NIH conducted a study where they compared lead versus mercury. They used Material Safety Data Sheets to aid them in their study. See the NIH Table on the next page.

As you can see from the NIH table on the next page, the health rating for lead is SEVERE while the health rating for mercury is EXTREME.

	Lead (Pb)	Mercury (Hg)
Description of toxicity	Poison, may be fatal if swallowed or inhaled	Danger! Corrosive, causes burns, may be fatal if swallowed or inhaled, harmful if absorbed through skin
Health rating	3—Severe (not on MSDS)	4—Extreme
Target organs/health effects	Irritation to skin, eyes, and respiratory tract, affects the gums, nervous system, kidney, blood, and reproductive system, possible cancer hazard	Kidney and central nervous system damage, allergic skin reaction
Symptoms of exposure	Abdominal pain, nausea, vomiting, headache, muscle weakness, "lead line" on gums, metallic taste in mouth, insomnia, dizziness, shock coma, death; with chronic exposure—irritability, visual disturbances, hypertension, gray facial color	Severe respiratory damage (if inhaled), shortness of breath, headache, muscle weakness, gastrointestinal disturbance, ringing in ears, death; with chronic exposure—muscle tremors, personality change, memory loss, metallic taste, loose teeth, skin rashes
Danger of cumulative effects (i.e., does exposure to small amounts over time build up in the body?) Yes or No	Yes	Yes
ACGIH threshold limit value[1]/time-weighted average[2] (TLV/TWA) (mg/m^3)	0.05	0.025

[1]Threshold limit value (TLV)—Estimated airborne concentration of a substance that a person can be exposed to at work without experiencing harmful effects. This does not consider other potential exposures of the substance outside of work or through diet.

[2]Time-weighted average (TWA)—An allowable exposure averaged over an 8-hour work day or 40-hour work week.

14

Just in case there's any confusion, extreme is far worse than severe. At the bottom of the table, this NIH study has also found that the exposure threshold for mercury is far less than it is for lead. Think about it, if you break one of the mercury, containing, fluorescent light bulbs, the manufactures of these bulbs will give you inhalation and clean up warnings. If your home has lead paint, it's recommended that you simply repaint. So, it appears as though a little bit of mercury can do a lot of damage. Just imagine, a little bit of mercury released near your brain, every day.

In January 2005, the Institute of NeuroToxicology and Neurological Disorders, regarding mercury, stated that 'Childhood disabilities from chemical exposure during development are often not treatable and therefore must be prevented.'

Now that we've discussed how toxic mercury truly is, I know you're as shocked as I was when I learned about amalgams. Mercury fillings? How could this be? Who would put mercury in people's mouths? Who would put mercury in the mouths of children? This has to be some kind of a sick joke, right? Where's the common sense?

I immediately started calling some of my friends and clients who work in the medical community. I found that many of them thought that these mercury fillings were no longer in use. Despite the fact that they worked in the medical industry, far too many of them knew nothing about the mercury in amalgams.

What do I do next? I decided to call my friends and family who didn't work in the medical community. Many of them had these fillings in their mouths and their children's' mouths. I didn't find one person who knew about the mercury. Not one! More importantly, I also didn't find one Mom or Dad who would have allowed these fillings to be placed in their child's mouth if s/he had known about its mercury content. **NOT ONE!**

I'm sure you're wondering how dentists can possibly get away with putting mercury fillings in the mouths of Americans, yet alone our children. Well, approximately 75% of Americans are unaware of the mercury content in their beloved 'silver fillings'. Ignorance is truly bliss. Americans can't fight against something that the majority of us don't know about or understand.

I'm often asked whether or not I sued the dentist who placed these fillings in KJ's mouth. Well, I called a few attorneys, but they were clueless. I knew more about these horrid fillings than they did. On top of that, amalgams are considered the 'standard of care'. I promise to tell you more regarding the 'standard of care' later in this guide.

Why didn't the dentist tell me about the mercury in these fillings? Why didn't he tell me that the mercury leaks? What happened to my right to informed consent? Informed consent is when a doctor gives you information about a drug, procedure or treatment so that you're aware of the side effects, risks and other factors. Again, I ask, where is my consultation or informed consent?

The few dentists, who have been kind enough to inform their patients about the mercury, tend to hide the disclosure in the fine print of paperwork that their patients sign. You know the paperwork I'm referring to; that large packet of information you have to fill out in order to become a patient. There is *rarely* any true informed consent regarding the danger of amalgams. Is there?

Do you know of a dentist who bluntly tells their patients that amalgams contain a leaking hazardous material? Do you think dentists will ever tell their patients what the Material Safety Data Sheet (MSDS) says about the amalgam product used by their office? It contains mercury and mercury is extremely toxic. Do some dentists put money above the safety of their patients? Dentists who use amalgams surely don't tell their patients that the mercury in the fillings leaks with normal use and wear and tear. Do they? Imagine this conversation with your dentist.

On the next page is the Material Safety Data Sheet MSDS for the Kerr-Sybraloy Amalgam, Precapsulated. As you can see, this particular product is approximately 44.5% mercury in weight. I won't fill the book up with a lot of material safety data sheets from various amalgam distributors, but you can stop by TheDumbPatient.com to see other amalgam MSDS examples. There are just far too many to place here.

MATERIAL SAFETY DATA SHEET

SYBRALOY, PRECAPSULATED

1 - IDENTIFICATION

Manufacturer: Kari Corporation
Address: 1717 Collins Ave.
City, State, Zip: Orange, CA 92867
Emergency: 1-800-626-4300
Telephone: Chemtrec 1-800-527-7823
Date Prepared: November 16, 2004

2 - COMPOSITION INFORMATION

Hazardous Ingredients

	CAS #	PEL	TLV	%
Mercury	7439-97-6	0.05 mg/m³	0.05 mg/m³	44.5*

* (%) based final Amalgam composition by weight.

Other Ingredients:
Alloy powder contains silver, tin and copper metals.

3 - PHYSICAL AND CHEMICAL PROPERTIES

Boiling Point: 634 °F
Specific Gravity (H₂O = 1): 13.55
Vapor Pressure (mm Hg): 0.0012 mm Hg @ 68 °F
Melting Point: -38 °F
Vapor Density: NR
Evaporation Rate: NR
Solubility in Water: 0.0002g/100g water @ 68 °F

Appearance and Odor: Powder. Odorless dark-grey alloy of silver, tin and copper. Liquid: Mercury is a silvery, mobile, odorless liquid.

This MSDS addresses the mercury (liquid) portion of the product, which is a known health hazard. The powder is not considered to be hazardous. The health hazard data section references information relative to individual quantities of elemental mercury and may not reflect the actual hazards of small quantities such as those encountered with this product.

4 - FIRE AND EXPLOSION HAZARD DATA

Flash Point (Method Used): N/A
Flammable Limits: LEL: N/A UEL: N/A
Extinguishing Media: Carbon dioxide, dry chemical foam.
Special Fire Fighting Procedures: Firefighters should wear self-contained breathing apparatus when fighting a fire in an area containing mercury.
Unusual Fire Fighting Procedures: Emits toxic fumes in fire conditions.

5 - REACTIVITY DATA

Stability: Stable
Conditions to Avoid: High temperatures
Incompatibility (Material to Avoid): Halogens, ammonia, and strong oxidizing agents
Hazardous Decomposition Byproducts: Mercury Vapor
Hazardous Polymerization: Will not occur

6 - HEALTH HAZARD DATA Acute/Chronic

Routes of Entry:
Skin: Irritant/Sensitizer (Neurotoxin/Nephrotoxin)
Acute Exposure: May cause redness and irritation. Chronic Exposure: Possible sensitization, dermatitis and swelling. Mercury may be absorbed through intact skin causing urinary problems.

Eyes: Irritant
Acute Exposure: Contact may cause irritation. Mercury is corrosive and may cause corneal injury or burns. Chronic Exposure: Mercury may be deposited in the lens of the eye, causing visual disturbances.

Inhalation: Irritant/Sensitizer/Neurotoxin
Acute Exposure: Inhalation of mercury vapor can cause fever, nausea, and vomiting. Chronic Exposure: Inhalation of high concentrations mercury vapor over a long period causes mercurialism. Findings are extremely variable & include tremors, salivation, stomatitis, loosening of teeth, blue lines on gums, pain & soreness in extremities.

Ingestion: Neurotoxin/Nephrotoxin
Acute Exposure: May cause nausea, vomiting, kidney damage and nerve effects. Chronic Exposure: Symptoms include Central Nervous System (CNS) disorders.

Carcinogenicity: NTP: No
IARC Monographs: No   OSHA Regulated Carcinogen: No

7 - EMERGENCY AND FIRST AID PROCEDURES

Skin: Wash thoroughly with soap and water. Use hand cream. If irritation persists, consult a physician.
Eyes: Flush with water for at least 15 minutes. Consult a physician.
Inhalation: Move to fresh air. If irritation persists, consult a physician.
Ingestion: Contact a physician. May cause neurotoxic/nephrotoxic effects.

8 - PRECAUTIONS FOR SAFE HANDLING & USE

Steps to be taken in case material is released or spilled. Isolate the area and begin clean-up immediately. Do not touch spilled material. Cover all liquid droplets with a commercially available mercury vapor suppressant such as HG-X or elemental sulfur. Collect the droplets using specialized mercury vacuum cleaner.

Waste Disposal Method: Material should not be allowed to enter sewers. All scrap mercury liquid and set alloy must be sent for reclamation by a commercial metal recycling facility.

Precautions to be taken in handling and storing. Store in a cool, dry place away from ignition sources. Other precautions: Use according to directions. Wash hands thoroughly before working or eating.

9 - CONTROL MEASURES

Respiratory Protection (Specify Type): Not needed for small quantities as encountered in this product. AVOID BREATHING OF VAPORS. HIGHLY TOXIC - IRRITANT - SENSITIZER.
VENTILATION:
Local Exhaust: Use in a well ventilated area to keep exposure under 0.05 mg/m³.
Mechanical (General): Should be sufficient
Other: Not Applicable
Protective Gloves: Chemical resistant or latex gloves required.
Eye Protection: Safety glasses with side shields. Full face shields.
Other Protective Clothing or Equipment: None
Work/Hygiene Practices: USE ONLY ACCORDING TO DIRECTIONS. Wash thoroughly after handling. Handle in accordance with good personal hygiene and safety practices. These practices include avoiding unnecessary exposure.

10 - TRANSPORTATION INFORMATION

Regulated: DOT, IATA, IMO
Proper Shipping Name: Mercury
Hazard Class: 8
UN Number: 2809
Packing Group: III
Label: Corrosive
NOTE: See 49 CFR 173.4

11 - SPECIAL INFORMATION

HMIS (Hazardous Material Identification System) Rating:
H1 F0 R0
[HMIS Index: 4 - Severe Hazard; 3 - Serious Hazard; 2 - Moderate Hazard; 1 - Slight Hazard; 0 - Minimum Hazard]

State RTK: California Proposition 65 WARNING: This product contains mercury, a chemical known to the State of California to cause birth defects or other reproductive harm.

Note: This MSDS was prepared in accordance with the requirements of the OSHA Hazard Communication Standard (29 CFR 1910.1200) and is to be used only for this product. The information in this MSDS is, to the best of our knowledge, believed to be accurate.

'Ok, Mom and Dad, I'm going to put amalgams in your daughter's mouth today. Now you should know that these fillings are an alloy that's 50% mercury by weight. Yes, mercury is one of the world's most toxic metals, but it's ok to use near the brain. We've been using it for over a century. Parents, don't worry about the mercury that leaks from her fillings when she eats chews or drinks her delicious hot chocolate. It's only a little bit of mercury. Yes, Mom, mercury is considered more toxic than lead and yes, as I already mentioned we're placing this filling in her mouth, near her brain. MOM, don't worry! So, would you like two mercury fillings or 3 for your daughter?'

Wow! Using mercury in anyone's mouth is so dumb it's not even funny. It defies all logic. I'm willing to bet that if a 5 year old knew what mercury was, s/he wouldn't want it in their mouths. I'm looking forward to the day when I walk into a dental practice and see a sign that says 'AMALGAMS CONTAIN LEAKING MERCURY!

Daily, I asked GOD for strength so that I could continue to educate myself regarding my son's healthcare. I needed to articulately speak the language of doctors so that I could properly advocate for KJ. I was scared. I was pissed! However, I had no choice but to remain calm. I wanted to know the truth, so every day I would read and read until I was exhausted.

Eventually, my research led me to other victims of mercury fillings like Freya Koss, Marie Flowers, Linda

Brocato, Dr. Dianne Meyers, and Dr. Dave Kennedy, D.D.S. retired and so many more. The people whom I've listed here have been diligently working to make the public aware of the hazards of mercury fillings for years. I reached out to speak with each of them. They all have a breadth of knowledge regarding mercury poisoning and amalgams. I soaked in the information they shared with me like a sponge.

KJ was chugging alone until March 2009. Things were about to drastically change. One day, KJ was walking up the stairs to go to his bedroom and he suddenly fell down. We weren't sure if he had tripped or lost his legs. He stood back up and everything appeared to be ok; until he fell again and again and again. Back to the hospital we go.

KJ underwent a nerve conduction study which led to a diagnosis of peripheral neuropathy in his lower extremities. His new mode of transportation became his wheelchair. It's critical for you to know that KJ went into the hospital walking, but days later, he was wheelchair dependent. Before this hospitalization, KJ was having difficulty walking, but nonetheless, he was still walking. Not one doctor had an explanation for the rapid deterioration of my son.

To make matters worse, they were kind enough to tell me that there was nothing that they could do for him. They expected that KJ would spend the rest of his life in a wheelchair, and at the pace he was deteriorating, they expected it to be a short life.

THE DOCTORS OF RADY'S CHILDREN'S HOSPITAL RENDERED THIS BLASPHEMY IN FRONT OF KJ! I WAS ABSOLUTELY PISSED! KJ WAS ONLY 15? WHAT KIND OF DOCTOR WOULD HAVE THIS CONVERSATION IN FRONT OF A CHILD?

Before discharge, they generously offered to set KJ up with outpatient physical therapy. I accepted and said, 'Send us home! I know what to do'. I really didn't, but KJ couldn't know that the mom he trusted and depended on was lost.

The next day, KJ was discharged from Rady's Children's Hospital of San Diego. I had to personally carry my son up the stairs, to his bedroom. I'm 5'6" tall and at the time I weighed about 120 pounds. My son was about 5'10", 145 pounds. When it was time carry KJ up the stairs, my Marine Corps training and instincts kicked in. He was wounded, and Marines NEVER LEAVE THEIR MEN (OR WOMEN) BEHIND!

I'm so proud of KJ. He's a fighter too. My handsome son is as strong as an ox. As long as I remained positive, in most instances he was positive too. We drew our strength from each other. Despite the pain he was enduring, KJ had a smile on his face every day. He's a comedian. He's always telling jokes and/or playing tricks on someone. You gotta love that attitude!

When KJ was in his wheelchair, he refused to move his bedroom to the lower level. Like most people who suddenly become wheelchair dependent, KJ wanted to be treated no differently than when he was healthy. We didn't run to get a handicapped plate for the car; we just planned for the positive future.

I didn't want KJ to label himself as handicapped. Words and descriptions are powerful. My son wasn't handicapped. We believed that this situation was a temporary setback. Sometimes KJ was able to crawl up the stairs on his own using his upper body strength.

Thank you GOD for allowing KJ to keep his upper body strength.

While staring at my son in a wheelchair, I knew that enough was enough. 'Ok, Taajah,' I said to myself. 'YOU'VE DONE ENOUGH RESEARCH!' It was time to get these disgusting mercury fillings removed from my son's mouth! They were killing him. I mean that literally. KJ was getting sicker and the doctors were still stuck in their *precious* medical journals trying to figure out why his disease was so active.

There were so many unexplained issues. By this time (March 2009), KJ had also acquired photo-sensitivity to light, rashes, and rapid heartbeat of 135 in his sleep. Trust me when I tell you that he had too many symptoms to list here. KJ's medical records even document tremors. I made my son sleep with me because his heart rate was so fast that I thought he would have a heart attack in his sleep. Thank GOD that he didn't.

Many of the aforementioned symptoms were blamed on the disease of lupus. Other symptoms were blamed on the medication he was taking. His rheumatologist at the time had the nerve to claim that KJ's tremors were due to a having bowel movement. She documented this in his medical records. I promise you that this was not based on a conversation. I have proof of her beliefs. I have medical records!

What's the importance of tremors? It's well known in the medical and mercury community that tremors are a sign of heavy metal poisoning. I once had a doctor tell me that if I had said that KJ had broken a thermometer with mercury, they would treat him for mercury poisoning because the symptoms were there. However, this doctor couldn't treat KJ for mercury poisoning regarding the fillings because there was no proof that amalgams contained enough mercury to cause harm. I firmly disagreed with the physicians. There's plenty of proof. Again, the proof isn't presented in their medical journals or medical schools, but the proof exists and is simple to find.

Sigh. Writing this guide is difficult for me. I have to re-live all of my hurt and agony that I experienced from watching my son suffers. Many, many times, I would ask GOD to let me take his place. I begged GOD to place his pain and burden on me. Breathe, Taajah. Breathe!

It's imperative that you understand that my baby boy was so ill. KJ's facial muscles were in so much pain that he had no control over his its movements. He was constantly drooling because he couldn't close his lips without using his hand. Once he let go of his lips, they would open back up. KJ had to drink from a straw in order to eat anything.

Yes, you're correct in your thinking. This meant that he could only eat certain foods. KJ was on an apple sauce and soft food diet by default. He even had to use his hands to hold his lips closed while simultaneously holding his head back in order to keep the food in his mouth so he could swallow. I thought my son was going to choke to death just from taking his medicine. I thank GOD that he didn't.

When I decided to have the fillings removed, KJ's doctors aggressively tried to talk me out of removal. They repeatedly warned me that removing this material could be even more dangerous to KJ's health. They wanted me to leave a material that was disposed of as hazardous waste in the mouth of my ailing son. This was the same toxic material that I knew was killing him. Well, that was my opinion. My beliefs were worthless to doctors. They were still in denial that the fillings had anything to do with KJ's poor health.

Now, his doctors were right about the removal of the amalgams. These mercury fillings have to be safely removed so that an excess amount of mercury doesn't enter your blood stream through the lungs. How stupid does that sound? What exactly is an excess amount of a highly toxic material? Is there such a thing as an excess amount of CRACK, COCAINE, LEAD or MERCURY? I ultimately found a great dentist on *www.IAOMT.org* whose dental practice did not use amalgams. Dr. Layton also followed all of the recommended safety protocols for removal of these horrible fillings. I didn't want to do any more damage to KJ.

KJ's mercury fillings were **safely** removed on Thursday, March 19, 2008 by Dr. Layton in Encinitas, California. Alas, but not to my surprise, KJ's photo-sensitivity to light, rapid heartbeat, tremors, rash, facial pain and lack of control of his facial muscles were all gone within a week. GONE! Yes, completely gone! **GOD IS GREAT!**

I couldn't wait to take KJ to see his doctors. Here's my proof that it was the fillings, right? Well, I'm sorry to inform you that his close minded doctors, book sense (not common sense) doctors claimed that the fact that these symptoms went away was merely a coincidence. They now believed that KJ's medicine was working. Rady's Children's Hospital of San Diego's doctors refused to consider the logical evidence and research despite all of the anecdotal evidence I provided them. My charts didn't matter. Again, I was ignored.

I remember that there had been times that his doctors blamed his symptoms on the medicine he was taking. Now they were saying that the medicine was getting rid of the side effects. Don't forget that they're talking about the same medicine that they earlier blamed as the cause for KJ's symptoms.

I know that I don't have a degree in medicine. However, if there was a degree for common sense, I would have a Ph.D.! So, for doctors to suddenly credit the medicines for the positive change was just plain stupid. At the end of the day, these doctors did anything and everything to ignore the fact that the only thing that had changed was the removal of the mercury fillings from KJ's mouth.

Now, even though some of KJ's minor symptoms had disappeared, you must keep in mind that KJ was still in a wheelchair and his neuropathy was getting worst. I was hoping it would be, but simply removing the fillings was not enough to reverse this 'neuropathy'. I finally had to accept that if my theory was right about the amalgams, KJ now has mercury stored in his tissues. He needed chelation therapy.

KJ was solely my responsibility. I had finally arrived at the conclusion that I would never get the help I needed in California, so, I decided that it was time to for us to pack up and try a hospital in another state. I was open to any hospital that would listen and research with an open mind! KJ and I were determined to travel the country to get him the medical care that he needed. I was tired of his current doctors practicing medicine on KJ. Their practice FAILED!

I had no choice but to do what most people considered extreme. When I made the decision to leave, KJ was on a 120mg of steroids a day! That's an obscene amount for anyone, yet alone a 15 year old child. It was

April, 2009 and he had been on that ridiculously, obscene dose since January, 2009. Something must be done and I couldn't wait for his doctors to do it.

OK. I know you're thinking that California is such a huge state that one would think that I shouldn't have to leave our home to get medical care. So, let me answer your question. Yes, I tried getting a second opinion in San Diego County; however when we arrived to the appointment with the new doctors, KJ's current doctors had already spoken to them. These doctors already had a preconceived notion regarding his diagnosis and even worst, regarding me. These doctors did a very basic exam and then complimented KJ's current doctors on their expertise. Even though these doctors were paid to give me a medical, second opinion they didn't even draw any of their own labs on KJ. It was a true waste of time and money.

KJ and I were left with no other options. I had to take my baby out of state to seek medical treatment. It was almost like we were running away from home. I had my savings and my consulting business. I told him that we might end up homeless in a tent, but I wasn't going to let him die or stay paralyzed. It was so depressing to see him so frail. He was getting so weak that we had no choice but to run away quickly. Time was of the essence.

Approximately one month later, we were on the plane to Memphis, Tennessee. We left with 6 suitcases (one was full of research) and a wheelchair for KJ. KJ

27

was far too weak to drive across the country. So, air had to be our mode of transportation. I had arranged for us to stay with the Hull family, a Navy friend, for two days until I worked out the hospital plan to get KJ admitted into a hospital.

April, 2009 was a scary time to go to the emergency room. If you can recall, this was during the time that the swine flu was spreading rapidly across the United States. KJ was already sick, so I was extremely hesitant to take him to any emergency room. Every emergency room across the country was packed with people coughing and wearing face masks. However, time was of the essence, so I had to take the risk. We went to the children's hospital and thank GOD that we had a nurse who understood how dangerous it was for KJ to sit in the emergency room with all of the potential swine flu patients. She put us in a small, private room until they were ready for us to see the doctor.

On April 30, 2009, K.J was admitted into Lebonheur's Children's Hospital in Memphis, Tennessee. My once healthy 15 year old son was severely frail due to losing 30 pounds. He lost this weight while taking 60 - 120 mg of steroids a day. When KJ started taking steroids, everyone told me to watch what he ate because he was going to gain weight. Steroids are supposed to make you gain weight. KJ was losing weight quickly, while on a high dose, with no logical explanation.

For 16 days, the doctors at Lebonheur's tried all

their conventional medicines and treatments for lupus, nephritis, and neuropathy. They poked, prodded and ran numerous labs and tests. Here we go again. Déjà vu! Haven't we been here before? While physicians were running their many tests, KJ was getting weaker and sicker by the moment. By this time KJ had lost the ability to stand, walk, or roll over in bed on his own. At night, when he wanted to roll over, he had to call me to his bedside for assistance. LORD, help him. No child should have to suffer like this? Why LORD, why?

Momma's baby couldn't even wiggle his toes and he was no longer ticklish under his feet. When KJ was healthy, if you pretended that you were going to tickle his feet, he would jump, run and automatically laugh. For those of you who are extremely ticklish under your feet, you know what I'm talking about. Now, you can only imagine how severe KJ's neuropathy had to be for this sensation to disappear.

This neuropathy was breaking KJ down and it was quickly spreading into his upper extremities. KJ could no longer use his upper body strength to go from the bed to his wheelchair. His upper body strength was almost nonexistent. I had to pick him up just so he could sit on a bedside toilet. I had to plead for him to fight for his life. There were days that he just wanted to give up. That's a lot to handle for a 15 year old child.

KJ was so weak at admission to the hospital that the doctors at Lebonheurs assigned him a physical therapist and an occupational therapist to try to strengthen his body. The main objective of the occupational therapist was to teach KJ ways to be independent in his wheelchair. They had various devices to help him do things like putting on his socks and shoes. He could barely bend over in his chair to even use these devices. I don't believe that anyone at Lebonheur's ever thought that they would see KJ walk again. I still believed. If I stopped believing, KJ wouldn't believe.

The entire time that KJ was in the hospital, I inundated Lebonheur's doctors with research. Every moment they were in his room, I took the time to share my information. Some doctors wouldn't listen, but I talked anyway. I was very, very adamant about being heard and I was extremely positive that mercury was the cause and inducer of KJ's ailments! I no longer cared about whether or not they thought that I was too aggressive. It was my intention to be just that. I surely wasn't going to be feeble with my requests. They really would have ignored me then.

The anecdotal evidence I presented to the doctors pointed to low dose chronic MERCURY poisoning. Yes, this mercury came from the fillings. Other than mercury poisoning, no one could justify the documented tremors! We could rule out that the tremors came from the medication, because he was still taking the medicine and since the removal of the amalgams, KJ no longer had tremors! To this day, no one ever has given me another reasonable explanation. I guess for some doctors, ignorance is bliss. Surely ignorance is cause for avoidance of the facts.

I often asked for and received hospital care conferences with KJ's hospitalist and his specialists. I pleaded and pleaded with them and ultimately convinced some of the doctors to do their own research. I even had them speaking to individuals like Dr. Boyd Haley, Ph.D. Dr. Haley had previously testified at an FDA board regarding the safety of mercury fillings and he successfully completed detailed research on this very issue. He is considered very knowledgeable regarding mercury fillings and poisoning.

The nephrologist at Lebonheur's was kind enough to ask her personal dentist about the mercury in amalgams. This dentist told her that I was wrong. He told her that the mercury was inert. I asked this educated nephrologist why she would take the word of the dentist when the ADA's website clearly states that a small amount of mercury leaks from the fillings. She never spoke of the issue again. She was never on board with anything that came out of my mouth.

On day 16 of our hospital stay, Friday, May 15, 2009, the attending doctor, Dr. Seveire (his hospitalist), entered the room and said that Lebonheur's Children's Hospital would treat KJ for mercury poisoning. This was the 1st day of the rest of KJ's life. As excited as I was, I remained cautiously calm. My Marine Corps discipline surely kicked in. I politely said, 'Thank you', and I began to review the literature for the drug they were using for the chelation.

31

Chelation therapy uses a drug that's designed to bind heavy metals (mercury, lead and others) together in order to assist the body in excretion of the toxin via urine. Typically the chelation drug is metabolized through the kidney, so I wanted KJ to receive this treatment responsibly. KJ had developed lupus nephritis (kidney disease) in January 2009, so I needed all the specialists to be involved in KJ's treatment for chelation. I needed him to be monitored in an inpatient setting versus an outpatient setting. That's why I fought so hard for KJ to receive chelation therapy in a hospital. Yes, I could have gone to many reputable, outpatient, alternative clinics for chelation, but that would have been my last resort.

Lebonheur's Children Hospital (or any American hospital that I could find) had never treated a patient for chronic low dose mercury poisoning due to amalgams. This hospital was very diligent in doing plenty research and they had multiple departments participating in the research. They wanted to ensure treating him with chelation therapy wouldn't do KJ more harm than good. I had a lot of respect for that line of thinking. Don't forget that it took 16 days of hospitalization for Lebonheur's Children's Hospital to agree to perform chelation therapy on KJ.

When Dr. Seveire told me that they were going to do the chelation, she also told me that I shouldn't expect any results from this treatment. Honestly, it was as if they were doing the treatment just because they had no other options. I don't think that they really did have other options. Conventional treatments had clearly failed.

Let's be frank here. I didn't care what their reason was, I was just thankful that GOD had made the treatment happen. We had done just about everything that the doctors asked of us. KJ's body was like a pin cushion. Nevertheless, chelation therapy for mercury poisoning began that Friday evening and continued the very next morning. Lebonheur's hospital chose to use DMSA for KJ's chelation therapy.

Before KJ and I left California, I was warned by many people who had tried to get chelation therapy treatment at a 'conventional' hospital that I was wasting my time. They told me that it couldn't and wouldn't happen. They told me to go and see an 'alternative doctor'. They said that I would never get a traditional hospital to treat him for mercury poisoning due to these fillings. Never say never to Taajah or a desperate mom. Never just wasn't an option.

On Saturday, May 16, 2009, (The morning after KJ's first dose of chelation), KJ and I went through our normal morning routine. As I did on every morning, I asked KJ if he could lift his leg while lying on his back in bed. To our surprise, KJ was able to lift his leg pretty high. Wow! Yeah! This was something he could not do the day, night, or week before. I was so excited and I couldn't wait for the doctor to come in and do their morning evaluation. Since it was the weekend, KJ did not have physical or occupational therapy. They were off on Saturdays and Sundays.

During his morning evaluation by the doctor on duty and KJ's nurse, KJ suddenly said, 'Wait a minute!' He grabbed his bedside table and rolled it over toward him. Shaking heavily, KJ miraculously was able to stand with the aid of his table! Yes, he was wobbly, but nonetheless, he did stand. The doctor and nurse looked shocked and dumbfounded. Heck, even I was dumbfounded. I was dumbfounded because I didn't expect to see results so quickly. Was this a miracle or was the treatment for mercury poisoning working? Maybe it was both. Thank you GOD! Thank you!

As you might have guessed, I was ecstatic. I was jumping around the room, crying and saying, 'Thank you Jesus'. It is documented in KJ's medical records that KJ's mom says that her tears are tears of joy. Well DUH! Of course they're tears of joys.

When KJ and I left California, I promised him that I would get him walking again. I promised him that he would not spend the rest of his life paralyzed in a wheelchair. Some people refuse to make promises to anyone. Yet here I was, telling my son that he would walk again. This was a very heavy promise and responsibility for me to keep. At times it looked impossible, but now my promise was coming to be. Faith is a powerful tool. Thank you Jesus! GOD was showing KJ favor! We had prayed. I had prayed. Now, watch GOD work!

On Sunday, May 17, 2009 (two days after treatment with DMSA began and one day after he was able to stand), KJ asked me to take him for a walk down the hospital hall. Go for a walk? Does my son need psychiatric treatment? Are all of these drugs making him crazy? I have to admit that I was totally confused by his request. Even though KJ had been able to stand yesterday, walking was a completely different story.

As a mom, of course I was concerned for his safety, but KJ insisted that he felt he could walk. The day before, after he had rested from standing, KJ and I tried to see if he could walk then. He was only able to take one shaky, weak step and it exhausted him completely. So, when KJ said that he felt like he could walk again, it seemed unrealistic and impossible to me. Nothing's impossible.

KJ insisted and I obliged! He wanted to walk while pushing his wheelchair down the hospital hall. So, per his request, I put my disbelief aside and I prepared KJ for his walk. To my surprise, he walked. Yes, he really walked. KJ pushed that wheelchair like he had been pushing it for weeks.

The nurses and other staff on the floor were amazed, excited, and joyful. I even saw a few tears from some of the ladies on staff. Per my request, one of the nurses took a picture of me walking behind KJ. I was walking behind him with my arms open so that I could catch him if he fell. He didn't fall. He barely even shook. The hospital hall was long, so KJ was too tired to walk back to his room, but who cared? I surely didn't. The staff didn't. KJ didn't care. He walked! Even if he had only taken 5 steps, it would have been a huge improvement. I can only imagine the joy that KJ felt after being able to walk down the entire length of the hall.

KJ was getting stronger by the moment. It's now Monday, April 18, 2009, so KJ is excited to show his physical therapist and occupational therapist his weekend progress. Before yesterday, my son hadn't walked in months and now he was talking about walking without the wheelchair. Of course you know that KJ was very excited. I think that he was too excited to cry. I rarely cried in front of him so I saved my soft tears for later that night while he was sleeping.

A couple of doctors still said that the correlation to walking and the treatment to mercury poisoning was a coincidence. Most of his doctors said nothing. More anecdotal evidence was thrown out of the window like a cigarette butt from a car window driving down the highway. Logic was simply dismissed because it didn't appear in their sacred medical journals.

To this day, the doctors at Lebonheur's Children Hospital NEVER did say what they believed to be the cause for KJ's sudden and remarkable recovery. The neurologist and nephrologist barely came into the room after KJ's miracle. It's like they didn't want to address the issue. In KJ's medical records, it's documented as to what I believe led to his KJ's recovery, but it's hard to find any detailed documentation as to what the doctors believed happened.

KJ's 'neuropathy' continued to improve and he was transferred from Lebonheur's Children's Hospital to inpatient physical therapy at Health South Memphis. Since he hadn't walked in months, he needed to strengthen his muscles in order to walk permanently without assistance. The physical therapist and nurses at Health South Memphis were great. The doctor...well let's just say that he missed an important diagnosis. It was important enough that I actually walked KJ out of the Health South unit and into the emergency room across the street to get the help that I knew he needed.

As I said, this is merely the beginning of KJ's story. There were more wars to fight to get us to the point that he's at today. Today, KJ is 19. KJ is walking, talking and living a normal life. He's playing basketball again and coaching at the local YMCA. He's preparing for college and getting ready to start training so that he can try out for a few college basketball teams. He recently grew 2 inches in about four months. He's now 6'3" tall, active and still growing.

Miraculously KJ has no signs of neuropathy. You can't look at him and tell that he was once paralyzed in a wheelchair. Although KJ began receiving chelation therapy on May 15, 2009, they didn't complete the chelation therapy (approximately one week) because the nephrologist at Lebonheur's found an excuse to end it. Her excuse...KJ had a tummy ache.

As I complete this guide, KJ has no *visual* or physical manifestations of lupus. Lupus is only (sometimes) diagnosed by his lab results. When I began navigating the healthcare system with my son in October, 2008, I was a **DUMB PATIENT**. I quickly learned and educated myself using all tools available to me. Now, my once seriously ailing and paralyzed son is walking, running, playing basketball and laughing. He's living a normal life. No wheelchair needed!

Remember, this is only the beginning and a small portion of KJ's Story. It's human nature to want to know why we have to experience certain things in life. I believe that I figured out the 'why'; the purpose. One purpose in life is to make sure that you and other families don't make the same mistakes that I did or the mistakes mentioned in this book. My purpose is to ensure that you and/or a loved one don't have to suffer unnecessarily.

This journey that you're about to take with me may cause you to cry, laugh and it should surely make you engage in self-reflection. You will never view your doctor's visit the same way. Get ready to take some notes. I'm going to take you from a **DUMB PATIENT** to a **SMART PATIENT**.

Chapter 2

What You Don't Know Might Kill You

We live in a world of immediate gratification. We want what we want now and we don't want to wait another minute, despite the future repercussions. Millions of families have accrued mountains of debt because they couldn't wait to get that 80" flat screen TV, Xbox 360 or some other material object. We ladies often perm our hair before it's time. Family members always sneak a bite to eat before dinner is completely done. Let's not forget to mention those hidden Christmas presents that you peaked at. Shhhh.

When it comes to immediate gratification, medicine is similar to life. We often ignore the potential long term, side effects in order to treat the current symptom. Who cares if the cold medicine will raise your blood pressure, as long as it allows you to breathe, **RIGHT NOW!** Since ignorance is bliss, most people never take the time out to even read the fine print of the drugs they use. It's kind of like ignoring the penalty and fees of the credit card used for that big purchase you couldn't afford.

In the grand scheme of things, there's one thing that we must always remember. Doctors are human! I could never drill this into your head enough. Most doctors mean well. They take their job seriously and they want to provide the best patient care that they can. KJ and I have had our fair share of great doctors.

Despite the Godlike and superior complex that some doctors appear to possess; they eat, breathe, dress, bleed and make mistakes just like you and me. Unfortunately, the mistakes doctors make can cost you your life or someone you love their life! With that said, there are many great doctors out there. Sadly, you may have to 'experiment' to find the one that's right for you and your family.

Now, throughout this guide, I could easily give you a list of resources that I want you to read in order to support my facts, but I want you to do your own research. Seek out the information yourself. If I say anything that's incorrect, just go to The **DUMB PATIENT** blog and let me know. Hey, I'm human and stats may change from month to month or year to year. Your goal here should be to learn from my experience. That also means that you must be willing to seek out the information you need. I want you to be a **SMART PATIENT** even when it comes to this guide.

Since knowledge is your friend, you should surely know that by the estimate of most experts, death by medical error will rank in the top 10 ways to die. Surprise! You are surprised, aren't you? The practice of medicine is polluted with medical mistakes. Since most patients don't take time to educate themselves about their own illness, yet alone the illness of a loved one, doctors are left to make the decisions for us. These patients blindly walk into a doctor's office and accept the diagnosis and prescription and then they leave for home. No profound questions are asked; if any are asked at all.

Statistics show that medical errors account for over 1,000,000 (one million) injuries per year. Approximately 200,000 deaths occur each year due to mistakes by doctors or hospital staff. Approximately 1.5 million Americans die, get sick or injured every year due to medication errors alone. These numbers do not include medical accidents, misdiagnosis or even failure to diagnosis or act. These numbers also don't include any 'unreported' errors.

If you walked into your doctor's office and there was a sign boldly placed in clear view stating that '**1. 5 MILLION AMERICANS DIE, GET SICK OR INJURED EVERY YEAR DUE TO MEDICATION ERRORS'**, I think that you would be more diligent with your visit. You would probably ask a few more questions about the drug you're being prescribed.

Let's be honest with each other. If your doctor told you your headache was from working too much and/or stress, what would you do? If you worked a lot or were stressed, you would take the prescription given and walk away. You probably wouldn't even think twice about it. Even if your doctor has been giving you the same diagnosis for years without any additional testing, you'll tend to believe him/her. Quick research shows that there are over 2000 diseases that can cause a headache. Is it stress, work related or something else? How many medications cause a headache? A **SMART PATIENT** will ask the right questions. They will also request labs if the problem persists.

Now, don't get all excited and start turning a headache into a life threatening disease that has you on your death bed. This was merely an example. It may even be a horrible example, but I needed to prove a point. You have to find the balance between being informed and being a hypochondriac or just plain psychotic!

Many **DUMB PATIENTS** believe that a doctor's education gives them the answer to all your ailments. All those years in medical school and all that training has to mean something, Right? Well, the World Health Organization (WHO) has recognized over 12,000 diseases. As of 2004, GenBank had placed over 22,000 diseases into various categories. WOW. What a disparity. There appears to even be disagreements as to what makes a disease a disease. In other words, the experts (usually physicians) even disagree. Keep in mind that for every disease, there's a 'specialist'. Getting to the right specialist, can be a long and daunting task.

Ask yourself this question, if medicine is always so cut and dry, why is there a need for a second opinion? Why do some doctors say a patient's life is over while another doctor will give the same patient options to live? Hey. I've been there with KJ. If I had listened to the California doctors, my son would still be in a wheelchair or I would have buried him by now. It makes me sick to my stomach to even say such a thing, but it's true.

Here's more food for thought. With everything being the same, why do different doctors prescribe different drugs (oops, I mean medicine) for the same disease? That's a great question Taajah. What's the answer? We'll discuss this issue in detail in another chapter.

OK, I digressed. To put this into some kind of perspective for you, let's use the conservative number of 12,000 known diseases as listed by the WHO. Typically your second level of defense is your primary care doctor. Second? Yes, **DUMB PATIENT!** You're your first line of defense! Geez!

Your primary care physician is supposed to coordinate your medical care and treat any illness that doesn't require a specialist. When it comes to medicine, the word 'treat' does not necessarily mean to cure. There are a lot of diseases that do not have what's called a 'known' cure. I smile as I tell you this, because there are many scientists, researchers and physicians who would disagree with that statement. They would probably say that there are known cures for most diseases, but since they aren't controlled by the pharmaceutical companies, they haven't been recognized. Some activists would say that many cures aren't discussed because there's more money and residual income in treating symptoms. Hey, I'm just putting the information out there. Don't shoot the messenger. I digress again. Sigh.

The field of medicine branches off into many specialties. It's the responsibility of your primary care to know which specialist to send you too. Sometimes, that can be a guessing game, based on your symptoms. Many illnesses share the same symptoms. How many of the 12,000 diseases do you think your primary care doctor studied in medical school? Do you even care? LOL. I know you care, but you're afraid to know the answer, aren't you?

Statistics show that a doctor spends approximately 5-7 (five to seven) minutes with you when you visit their medical practice! OH! Let me digress. It's called the practice of medicine. YES! **THE PRACTICE OF MEDICINE!** When doctors make mistakes, many of them blame it on the science. 'It's not a perfect science,' some will say. Many physicians even say that it's more of an art. Yet, when we remind them that they should keep an open mind because it's an imperfect science and an art, they're offended. Is it just me or is that a double standard favoring doctors?

Let's finish discussing your much needed office visit to your doctor. During your 5-7 minute visit, you should receive a brief examination. This probably includes ears, eyes, nose, throat, chest, breathing…the basics.

I won't bore you with all the details. You know the routine. Mostly, gone are the days of receiving personal attention from your doctor. Yes, there are exceptions to the rule, but personal attention is not the rule of thumb anymore. If you have a doctor who will take their time and render to you extended personal attention at your appointments then, count your blessings! These doctors are the exception, not the rule.

KJ's current rheumatologist, Dr. Hayes of Piedmont Hospital in Atlanta is one of those rare specialists who will take his time with his patients. I clearly recall our first appointment with Dr. Hayes. I was burning with anger because he ran so late beyond our appointment time. I felt insulted. Hey, my time is valuable too. His tardiness caused me to have to cancel my business appointments. When I tell you that Dr. Hayes was late, I'm not talking about only 30 minutes late. He was literally a couple of hours late. After doing my deep breathing exercise, I eventually learned to appreciate the fact that when he came in the room to speak with KJ and me, Dr. Hayes would take his time with us too. He never rushed us out of the room until our questions were answered and needs were met. I did learn how to work within his system. I now try to get the first a.m. appointment so we don't catch the buildup at the tail end of Dr. Hayes' day.

The length of time that a patient spends with their doctor has decreased significantly over the years. We have all heard wonderful, old school stories from our elders of doctors who used to visit the homes of their patients. Yes, those were the good old days. We have also heard about the personal relationships that our forefathers had with their doctors. Unless your doctor is a friend or family member, do these relationships exist anymore?

I'm a business woman so I truly understand the reality. **MEDICINE IS A BUSINESS!** As a business, medical practices need to be profitable too. Over the years, I've done business consulting and Continuing Education Units (CEU's) seminars for many physicians and medical practices across the country. When my clients medical offices were not profitable, I recommended the addition of more patients and services to their practice. At the end of the day, it's my job to put my clients on the road of profitability. I'm great at my job. Maybe too good. I now realize that I contributed to the healthcare problem. I'm very sorry for my role! I have learned that healthcare can't just be about the bottom line. Healthcare can't just be about profit and losses. Many doctors have forgotten that the word **CARE** is in healthcare!

Let's focus on your doctor visit. Although the amount of time that you spend with your doctor has decreased, on the other hand, time spent in the waiting room has increased significantly and healthcare costs have risen. You must understand that it doesn't cost a medical practice any money to have you sit in the waiting room or exam room and read a magazine. When it comes to waiting and our time, there's another double standard. It's really a tad unfair too. See, if the patient is late, certain medical practices will require you to pay a fee for being late and/or the appointment may be cancelled and rescheduled. Also, if you cancel with less than 24 hours to your appointment, they still may charge a fee. When doctors cancel your appointments, as a patient, you just suck it up and rebook the appointment for a later date. You get an apology, but you have to deal with the cancellation or go to another doctor.

Even if your doctors use the seven minute visit rule, how many of them are ever on time? The staff of physicians' offices is notorious for booking multiple appointments for the same time slot. Most doctors are always in a hurry to move on to the next patient. More patients mean more money. 7 minutes is barely enough time to read a menu in a new restaurant so it is very unreasonable to expect a patient to understand even the basics of their health in that 7 minutes. However, this has become business as usual.

The **DUMB PATIENT** has been trained by doctors to not question short doctor visits. They're just happy to get an appointment. The **DUMB PATIENT** thinks a short doctor's visit is normal and reasonable. Plus, we're a society who's always in a rush, so we often think that a short visit benefits us, the patient. When a **SMART PATIENT** with questions walks in, some doctors can become impatient. The **SMART PATIENT** tends to be labeled as difficult, crazy and unreasonable.

Many doctors get extremely aggravated when questioned. They're insulted and that often leads to them losing patience. I can only imagine what they're thinking. How dare a layman question my authority and knowledge? I really don't have to imagine, I've personally been told that. First, they ask me if I'm a nurse or doctor. When they find out that I'm 'just a MOM', they're insulted. I've had doctors chant things like, 'This is my specialty. I have been prescribing this drug for many years,' etc. The **DUMB PATIENT** has made it difficult for the **SMART PATIENT** to hold doctors to realistic expectations.

Here's an analogy. Just imagine ordering a surf and turf dinner at a 5 star restaurant. You are so excited to eat this delicious tender lobster and steak because many people you know have given the chef rave reviews. For weeks, your mouth has been watering for a medium rare filet mignon with perfectly steamed vegetables, so you order your dinner with enthusiasm. Yum! Yum! Upon receiving your meal from your server, you're disappointed to find that your overpriced, expensive steak is overcooked and barely warm. You asked for medium rare and you received a tepid, medium well steak of poor quality. You question yourself, 'Do I have the right restaurant?'

You glance around the room and you see many people chewing what appears to be very tough steak. Either they all ordered their steak well done or, 'Houston, we have a problem.' You even hear the table next to you quietly complain about their meal amongst themselves as they are dining, but they continue to eat the food anyway. Now, you and your date realize that there are many unhappy customers, but no one is sending there meal back. No one says anything.

Disgusted and disappointed, you call for your server and kindly explain that your steak is cold and overcooked. With a slight attitude, she removes the meal from your table. Suddenly, your expectation of excellence appears unreasonable because the other diners did not speak up. Is everyone else happy or are they just quietly trying to get through their dinner?

I have to admit, I have quietly consumed a meal that wasn't up to my standards before. We've all heard horror stories about what the kitchen staff might do to your food when you send it back to the kitchen. So, out of fear of the unknown, we sometimes say nothing. Expecting hot food is a valid request. It shouldn't matter whether you are at a 5 star restaurant or a fast food, drive through; restaurants that don't provide great customer service are angry when you question the quality of their food.

What happened in the restaurant example is often the same silence we see in a doctor's office when patients are dissatisfied. There's a huge difference between silence in a restaurant and saying nothing to your doctor. In medicine, your silence can be deadly. In healthcare your silence can cost you your life. With that said, your doctor should be willing to discuss your health and your concerns in detail regardless of your ethnic, age or educational background. S/he should be willing to spend a reasonable amount of time with you. What is reasonable? I personally think that reasonable is when your concerns are answered.

Sorry, but I can't define what's reasonable for your situation. You have to define that for yourself. Just don't let your doctor make you feel badly because you want to be involved in the decisions concerning the healthcare of you, your child or your loved one. Don't let him/her rush you out of their office when you still have questions that are unanswered or answers that you don't understand. As a patient, you do have rights. Also, doctors also have an 'oath' to uphold.

WHAT YOU DON'T KNOW COULD KILL YOU! Follow your instincts and research, research, research. Research carefully and use common sense. Remember, that headache could be just because of stress.

Now, I have to warn you that doctors hate it when a patient tells them that they have researched on the internet. Based on my experience, most doctors are not fans of Google. Doctors like to pretend that every website you visit on the internet has inaccurate information. Some websites do contain inaccurate information, so you must be aware of the source of the website and information, but many of the medical websites were created by doctors and they also have medical doctors as advisors and/or board members.

When I was doing my research for KJ, most of his doctors gave me smug looks when I tried to share the information that I had printed out. Some wouldn't even take it in their hands. It was like the papers that I was presenting to them were laced with some kind of disease that's worse than the plague. Mind you, that my son was paralyzed and rapidly getting sicker. I would think that everyone would be on board with any help that they can get.

KJ's doctors were far from open-minded. One doctor even told me that I was obsessed with mercury! Obsessed? You're darn skippy I'm obsessed. My obsession was simple, reasonable and logical. I was obsessed with getting doctors to review ALL information so that my son could walk again and get back to being a teenager.

I never had tunnel vision. I personally was never married to the mercury concept. However, I did expect the doctors to eliminate their tunnel vision and be willing to use their peripheral vision to pursue other options. I just needed and expected them to accurately, thoroughly and professionally address the mercury issue. There was nothing to lose. What the doctors were doing wasn't working, so why not listen to the parent!

Trust me; I quickly learned that you have to be bold enough to let your doctor know that you expect him to answer your questions. If your doctor doesn't have the answers to your questions, then s/he MUST refer you to another doctor who may. There's absolutely no compromising here! You must believe that your life and the life of your loved one is valuable and worth advocating for.

After you've tried to get the proper assistance and service from your doctor and you still feel that the care you're receiving is inadequate, tell someone. Comprise a formal letter to the doctor's hospital administration and/or the medical board. Doctors often repeat the same mistake if it isn't addressed. While you're writing your letter, don't forget to find another doctor!

Recently, I was speaking with a lady whose daughter has been very ill. She started describing the complications she was having when communicating with her daughter's doctors. She then began to tell me details about one particular doctor who was ignoring some of the side effects of a particular medication. Although the side effect that her daughter was experiencing was clearly listed on the drugs MSDS issued by the drug company, the doctor still insisted that he had never seen this actual side effect in one of his patients. This doctor negated the possibility that he was viewing this side effect in this particular patient. This desperate mother went on to say that this doctor was accusing her daughter of not taking her medicine.

STOP THE PRESSES! Is it possible that I may know this doctor? I bluntly asked the lady if the doctor she was speaking of was the pediatric nephrologist, Dr. Williams with Our Lady of the Lake Hospital in Baton Rouge, Louisiana. 'Of course it was,' she replied. The story that this mom shared with me was all too familiar. Dr. Williams had used the same tired lines and explanations on me for some of KJ's issues.

I told you in Chapter 1 that my son, KJ, still has a diagnosis that doctors call lupus. In January 2010, KJ was looking different to **ME** (not his doctors). I couldn't put my finger on it, but my 'maternal instinct' told me that something was very wrong. KJ's primary care (at that time) was not very good at coordinating care. She would write down a couple of names and phone numbers of specialists and practically leave me to fend for myself. She was the epitome of the unspoken 7 minutes rule. She gave us 7 minutes (if we were lucky) and out the door we were.

When KJ was looking 'different', I called Dr. Williams and left several messages for him to call me back, ASAP. I practically begged him to return my call. Day 1, 2 & 3, I heard nothing from him. I knew why he wasn't returning my calls but I was hoping and praying that his ego wasn't so big that he would allow my son to suffer. I'm sure that Dr. Williams had taken the 'Do No Harm' oath.

See, Dr. Williams was upset with me because I took the advice of another specialist (KJ's rheumatologist at that time) over his advice. HA! Did we get different medical advice for the same problem? No way! That wouldn't happen. Would it? Of course I'm being facetious.

You should know that the advice from the rheumatologist was the complete opposite of what I had received from Dr. Williams, the nephrologist. The rheumatologist whose opinion differed from Dr.

Williams even put it in writing via a letter to me and copied Dr. Williams. The rheumatologist clearly stated and explained why his treatment plan differed. OH yeah. He also stated Dr. Williams' name right in the letter! OOOOH. What drama. Hollywood couldn't make this stuff up.

Anyway, Dr. Williams and I were already having communication issues because I went against his advice. It's my opinion that he wanted me to do things his way or the highway. He never said that, but actions speak louder than words. From his viewpoint, there was no discussion needed regarding anything. Dr. Williams also had the bad habit of wanting to play the role of many specialists in one; rheumatologist, nephrologist, psychologist and teacher. Most importantly, he kept claiming that the reason KJ was sick was because he had not been taking his medicines.

When Dr. Williams did not return my calls, I followed my maternal instincts and I drove my son 1.5 hours away from Baton Rouge, to the children's hospital in New Orleans. THANK GOD I did! KJ had life threatening hyperkalemia (high potassium level) of 9.5 and 10 mEq/L. At most hospitals, a normal potassium level is considered 3.5 to 5.0 mEq/L. KJ's potassium level was double the norm. Do your research and let me know on **THEDUMBPATIENT.com** what the odds are of having and surviving a 9.5 and 10 potassium level is.

According to the physicians at the hospital, my son should have had a cardiac arrest and died because his potassium levels were so high. According to GOD, KJ is needed here on earth, so ordinary circumstances don't seem to apply to him. New Orleans Children's Hospital had to insert a temporary line in KJ's leg in order to administer emergency dialysis. Dialysis is given to a patient to clean the blood of toxins when the kidney isn't doing the job properly. In KJ's case, his potassium level was so high dialysis was needed to help the kidney eliminate the potassium quicker. KJ quickly recovered and was discharged home.

During the time that KJ was in Intensive Care Unit (ICU) preparing for this emergency dialysis, I was able to finally get the long lost Dr. Williams on the phone. The assistant who answered this call seemed to be frustrated that he hadn't phoned me back. She still remained professional, but I could hear it in her tone. While KJ was undergoing emergency dialysis, Dr. Williams continued to deny the possibility of a 9.5 potassium level. I asked him to call and speak with the nephrologists at Children's Hospital. He never did. Darn EGO! Of course, we dropped Dr. Williams as KJ's nephrologist like a smelly, rotten sack of potatoes!

Due to the high potassium levels, changes were made to KJ's medicine! See, KJ was on two ace inhibitor drugs called Enalapril and Cozaar. This is important because these two drugs can increase the potassium levels in your blood. Hmmmm. Let's think this through. I guess that high potassium wouldn't have been an issue if KJ had really stopped taking his medicines. Just proof that Dr. Williams was wrong.

Imagine being 16 and a medicine that's supposed to keep you healthy almost contributes to your death. I'm sure that you can understand that after the potassium incident, KJ really didn't want to take any medications anymore. KJ wanted to know why he was taking drugs that were only making him sicker. That's a great question, KJ. Mommy is still working on that answer.

What's my point to this story? It's my opinion that Dr. Williams followed an obvious pattern. I personally don't believe in coincidences, so if he is using the same tired lines and practices on someone I happen to randomly discuss medical care with, what are the odds that he's using it on other patients? The odds are EXTREMELY HIGH!

What's a patient to do? You have the responsibility to report any substandard care you receive to the administrative staff of the hospital or the medical board. Reporting substandard care may seem trivial when you're fighting for the life of a loved one. I didn't know better at the time. So, as soon as you can, make it a priority to file the report. Your actions may save a life of someone else.

Chapter 3

Your Glorified Drug Dealer

Let's play a multiple choice game and you must pick one of the following choices. Don't cheat! Here's the question: Which disease do you want to get; diabetes, high blood pressure, neuropathy, glaucoma, impotence, infertility, rashes, osteoporosis, weight gain, weight loss, headaches or glaucoma? How about an autoimmune disease like lupus or maybe even a liver or kidney disease? Oooh! I think I know the answer. Do you want CANCER?

No, my friend, I'm not crazy (unless you think sky diving, bungee jumping or cliff diving into shark infested waters in Hawaii is crazy). Wink. Wink. The disease options I offered you sound ridiculous right? Which disease did you pick? None of them? Why? O.k., be honest. Have your ever taken the time to completely read the side effects, contraindications and/or the MSDS for the drugs you or your loved ones are taking? There are many serious diseases and illnesses that can be caused by various prescription drugs.

I was recently speaking with a friend who has high blood pressure. He's a single dad and not the greatest cook so he dines out frequently. Like many bachelors, he mostly frequents fast food restaurants. One day KJ and I was on the phone explaining to him the sodium content in the various fast foods he was eating. KJ had to learn this information when he was put on a sodium restricted diet. The sodium content, fat, etc. of food is easy to find because the restaurants MUST publish it on their websites or some other source so consumers may easily obtain the information.

So, of course I asked my friend if his doctor had ever sent him to speak with a nutritionist. No was the answer. Ok, did the doctor ever even mention a nutritionist to him? Emphatically, he said, 'No!' He was simply asked if there was high blood pressure in his family and told that his disease was hereditary. The doctor wrote out a prescription for a high blood pressure medicine and sent him on his way. It was obvious that his pressure was high on that day so, my friend didn't ask his doctor any questions.

Of course I'm not a doctor and in no way is **THE DUMB PATIENT** designed to give you any medical advice. Our purpose is to educate you so that you have a system to assist you in navigating this complicated healthcare maze. However, from a common sense perspective, why wouldn't the diet be the first consideration and change that his physician would make to/for my friend? Let's say that his blood pressure was so high that he needed medication immediately, why not give him a prescription along with a consult to speak with a nutritionist? Even with the drugs, wouldn't it also be necessary to discuss a dietary change. Think about it and let me know your opinion on **THE DUMB**

PATIENT's blog.

Here's another example for you to consider. I took my Mom (Mary) to the doctor for her yearly physical. When her doctor received the results from my Mom's labs, it showed that my Mom's Low Density Lipids (LDL) was about 4 points out of whack. What do you think the doctor did with those results? You got it. The kind and knowledgeable doctor prescribed a statin (a class of drug used to lower cholesterol levels) while failing to discuss any dietary changes or retesting to see if her cholesterol level was actually normal.

My question is simple. Why are most doctors so quick to write a prescription for a drug that may do more harm than good? Why are drugs their first line of defense when there may be other viable and logical courses to take?

My son has been prescribed so many unnecessary drugs that I had to teach KJ to not take any medication that he didn't recognize and to make the nurse tell him the names and purpose of any new medications. That's a lot for a teenager to have to do, but after almost receiving the wrong medication on several occasions, KJ understood the necessity of this step. If the nurse tried to give him a new medication and I was out the room, he always said, 'Please wait for my mom to get back.' Usually I was right there with KJ while he was in the hospital. Of course there were times that I was out of his room briefly in order to go to the cafeteria, store, visit a client, etc.

In my humble, layman's opinion, the most overused drug type is antibiotics. Again, don't take my word for it. Research the information for yourself. Antibiotic resistant infections are on the rise. The CDC has an article called '*Antibiotics Aren't Always the Answer*'. I've had to turn down antibiotics on numerous occasions because the doctors were prescribing them to KJ when they really didn't know what else to do. Thank GOD that I was right. As fate would have it, KJ didn't need those antibiotics after all.

To add insult to injury, over the past few years of KJ's illness, I have personally caught hospitals administering wrong IV's, medications, doses, etc. I have spoken to other parents whose children were in the hospital and it saddened me to say that many of these parents were the personification of a **DUMB PATIENT!** Parents are surely not **DUMB PATIENTS** intentionally. Doctors have practically brainwashed many patients to not question their authority. Many doctors attempt to make you feel as if they are smarter than you because they attended a University longer and they have a title with initials attached to their name. Many doctors consider a patient to be belligerent when s/he questions the choices of their physician. Remember, you can only be belligerent to someone who's superior to you.

Question. What do you call a doctor who finished last in medical school? A doctor! Ha ha ha ha ha! We, as patients are never informed about our doctors grades or if they 'barely passed' their exams and classes.

Doctors don't wear their grades or class standings on their white coat, but they should. We don't know how well or how poorly they did in medical school and residency. Boy oh boy would I love to know the class rankings of a few doctors I've encountered.

There have been multiple times that I had to turn down a medication that the doctor had no reasonable explanation for prescribing to KJ. Maybe they misread a symptom or thought that they heard a symptom that was never said. Who knows? I don't! Sometimes, doctors could barely tell me the side effects of the drug they were prescribing or give me other medication options for KJ. This particular drug that they were prescribing was all they knew and sometimes that knowledge was debatable. Of course, when I questioned them or showed genuine concern for KJ (sometimes confusion), I was labeled as a difficult parent, but so what! Label me! I didn't care and I still don't.

So, the title of this chapter is 'Glorified Drug Dealer'? I can hear you saying, 'Taajah, aren't you being a bit harsh?' No. I refuse to apologize for calling things as I see it. Heck, as a Marine, I fought for free speech of others, now I'm utilizing the right that I fought for. I do understand that with free speech comes responsibility. Thus, I'm responsibly informing you that drugs can kill or injure.

I know I'm truly angering many people who sincerely believe in the safety and efficiency of the United States healthcare system. I have no concern about making friends or enemies. My number one care is about the health of my son. My secondary concern is educating others so that a life can be changed or saved. I can only tell anyone who's angry about this guide that I'm open to debating the content of **THE DUMB PATIENT** anytime, anywhere and with anyone. Hawaii would be preferred.

Let's get back on track. The CDC reports that almost half (1/2) of Americans are on some kind of prescription medication during any given month and this percentage continues to increase. Yes, this sad number includes our children. Have you ever wondered how your doctor chooses a particular medication that they prescribe to you? I know what you're thinking... Doctors do tons of research and comparisons to choose the right drug for your illness and/or situation. Right? Unfortunately, in most cases, they don't! Yes, some do, but many (probably most) don't.

Keep in mind that I don't drink, smoke or use 'recreational' drugs or support its use. However, I was very surprised to find that in the United States there are more deaths and complications from prescription drugs than street drugs. Yes, I'm sure that you're as shocked as I am. Aren't you? Then again, maybe you already knew these numbers. If that's the case, you aren't shocked at all.

I've always wondered: How do many doctors choose the drugs they prescribe? I sadly learned that while a student is in medical school they spend less than

5% (approximate) learning about drugs and prescription writing.

Let's explore this. Have you ever been to your doctor's office and noticed a pen or pad with a drug company's name on it? Of course you have. I'm sure that the pen and pad fairy didn't bless your doctor with an abundance of free gifts. Those pens and pads are the wonderful marketing efforts of the powerful and wealthy drug companies. Pharmaceutical companies (drug companies) use a variety of tools to market their drugs to your doctors.

Realistically, if someone came to my office and dropped off a bunch of pens and pads, I might be more likely to recommend their product to my clients. However, my products don't KILL people or lead to other diseases.

I know what you're probably thinking. A pen and pad is really harmless, isn't it? Keep in mind that pharmaceutical companies spend billions of dollars a year wining, dining and 'educating' doctors and the public about their drugs. Some practicing doctors even receive cash payments to 'educate' other doctors about a particular drug.

Many doctors claim that the drugs that they decide to use is not related to the marketing practices of drug companies. Take a moment to ask yourself this point blank question. Would pharmaceutical companies spend approximately $20,000,000,000 (20 billion dollars) a year in marketing products to doctors and the public, if their marketing strategies didn't work. Pharmaceutical companies spend this money on marketing because they know that most doctors will prescribe the drugs that they see and hear about more often. Point blank! Drug companies spend more on marketing than they do on research and development. Sigh.

Ex-pharmaceutical reps have shared many drug company tactics. They mention rewards and benefits to doctors who will promote their drugs. Drug reps often provide 'free' samples to doctors as an enticement for their patients. Hmmm. How many 'free' drug samples have you ever received? How many free samples have you ever requested? That's more food for thought, right? I know you're thinking now. When was the last time you were able to watch TV without seeing a commercial about a prescription drug? My goal is for you to walk into your doctor's office educated and with your eyes open.

Most doctors get their pharmaceutical drug information directly from the drug companies themselves. This courtship can often begin as early as medical school and the courting never, ever ends! Yes, some institutions have put restrictions on how drug companies can market to their staff, but aggressive restrictions are not found in the majority of medical practices and hospitals.

It's well known that many medical schools receive grants and 'gifts' from pharmaceutical companies.

Sometimes, drug companies provide the small curriculum used to educate medical students about their own drugs. Pharmaceutical companies practically teach doctors what they want them to know regarding their drug. Sweet, right? How can drug companies get away with that? It's easy. When you have a powerful lobby, buying and paying for elections, you can accomplish much in America. Yep, I said it. Sad isn't it?

You should also know that deaths from medications can often mimic deaths from natural causes. So the staggering numbers we are about to discuss are from **KNOWN** cases only. You already saw some of the numbers relating to medical error in chapter 2. We will discuss those numbers in more detail here. Pay attention and you will never be a **DUMB PATIENT** again!

Approximately 1.5 million Americans die or are injured every year in hospitals due to medication errors alone. These numbers do not include medical accidents, misdiagnosis or even failure to diagnosis or act. More people die yearly from pharmaceutical drugs than all the street drugs combined!

Stop the presses! Aren't prescription drugs approved by the FDA? How can we have so many deaths and errors from prescription drugs in AMERICA? If we are going to discuss doctors and drug companies, I would be re-missed in my duties if we didn't discuss our beloved government (FDA) and their relationship with pharmaceutical companies. Hold on a minute. I'll be right back. I need to get my Marine Corps flak jacket

65

before I go on. I may need to be bulletproof because it's about to get really sticky around here.

Your precious FDA was created to protect consumers. Right? Yet the FDA DOES NOT DIRECTLY TEST THE DRUGS that they APPROVE. THEY DON'T DIRECTLY or INDIRECTLY (via an independent organization) TEST THE DRUGS THAT THEY TELL US, THE GULLIBLE AMERICAN PUBLIC, ARE SAFE!

What? Are you shocked, again? What exactly do I mean when I say that the FDA doesn't directly or indirectly test the drugs they approve? How can the FDA approve a drug that they have never, ever tested, you ask? Who does the testing? Is the testing done by an independent panel of scientists or doctors? Ah. My curious one. The answers you seek may not be the answers that comfort you.

It gets much worse. Many of the board members of the FDA have conflicts of interest regarding the drugs that they rule on. The FDA's board members are not restricted from consulting with, owning stock of, etc. of drug companies while they're active on the FDA board. This system is laced with trouble and greasy palms.

In 2009, Attorney Charlie Brown of Consumers for Dental Choice wrote a complaint to the Inspector General of the United States to discuss the conflict of interest that Dr. Margaret Hamburg (head of the FDA) maintained while sitting on an FDA board hearing to discuss the safety of amalgams. Dr. Hamburg owned a significant amount of shares in one of the top amalgam providers. If the FDA ruled against amalgams, the stocks of amalgams were destined to decline. After the FDA ruled in favor of amalgams (mercury fillings), the CEO of a large amalgam company announced appreciation to Dr. Hamburg for her 'insights'.

Let's put the FDA's drug approval system into perspective. If I was kind enough to recommend a babysitter for your child, one would realistically 'assume' that I have personally tested (ooops, used) this babysitter for my child in the past. If you hired this babysitter and had a terrible experience, you would surely come to me to discuss the problems you had with him/her. You would want to know if you had bad timing and whether or not the bad service rendered was a one-time experience. Maybe it was just a fluke or does this babysitter need to be recalled (I mean fired). You would pose a logical question to me, 'How come she was so great with your child, but so horrible with mine?'

How would you then feel when you found out that I had never tested (ooops, used) him/her to babysit for me? How would it make you feel to know that I placed your children at risk based on the positive feedback that I received directly from the babysitter him/herself? Hey, s/he told me that s/he was a good babysitter. I reviewed the data that s/he provided. It looked like s/he was more likely to be good than bad, so I approved (I mean believed) him/her.

In my humble opinion, what we have with the FDA and the drug approval process is very similar to the babysitter analogy we just discussed. Yes, the FDA does review the drug company's data, but as I understand it, the data is submitted by the drug companies themselves. They complete their own research on the products they develop. Pharmaceutical companies monitor their own trials (or pay someone to do it) and then submit the results to the FDA. Does this process make any kind of ethical and/or logical sense to you? When you consider the many drug recalls we've had in the United States lately, are you comfortable with this drug approval process?

I reiterate. The pharmaceutical companies are responsible for conducting the testing and research of the drugs that they want to have approved and then the drug companies submit these results to the FDA! This almost sounds as if the pharmaceutical companies are 'practically' policing themselves. SWEET!

Here's another analogy. How many students would be on the honor roll if they were allowed to check and grade their own papers! How many Ph.D.'s and M.D.'s would we have then? Doesn't this go against everything we have been taught in our precious educational system (that's a whole different can of worms)?

Ask yourself these questions. Can a drug company honestly submit unbiased results about the drugs that can make them millions, billions or trillions of dollars? Doesn't the submission of positive results lead to the drug being approved by the FDA? Since FDA's approval will help determine the financial health of these drug companies, the value of its stocks and of course, the happiness of shareholders, can pharmaceutical companies really be trusted to be unbiased and honest with the data they submit. Hey. I'm just asking and providing information. You have to decide for yourself!

In October, 2012, many people across the U.S. became sick from tainted steroid injections. In this particular case, the tainted drugs are blamed on a pharmacy that does compounding. Yes, this is different than a drug recall by a pharmaceutical company, but it surely goes to the heart of the matter. It's my understanding that this pharmacy has slid under the radar and has gone without the proper FDA inspections for years.

In my humble opinion (I say this often); the FDA has not always been very effective at doing their job. Are they understaffed? I don't know. What exactly is the job of the FDA? As I understand it, the FDA is supposed to provide the first layer of protection regarding drugs, food, implants and devices for the American public.

Here's another perspective. Imagine a criminal sitting on the jury of his trial. What do you think the verdict would be in the majority of cases? Could this legal system ever be truly effective in America? Would you convict yourself to life in prison or the death penalty if the final vote was yours? Be honest! Would this system protect or benefit the good of the public or the good of the criminal?

It's time to make some changes. When you're prescribed a medication, you have to ask your doctor questions such as:

1. *Why are you prescribing this drug versus a similar medication?*

2. *How long has this drug been used for this disease?*

3. *Why are you prescribing this dose?*

4. *What are the side effects?*

5. *What are the contraindications?*

6. *Will you please give me the MSDS in writing?*

7. *Is there another option for treatment that does not require a drug?*

Here's another question. A lot of money goes into finding cures for some of the worst diseases, but where are all the cures? Don't forget that there is a difference between treating a symptom and curing a disease. What's the difference? Residual income! How much of our tax money actually goes into funding research for drugs? I stated earlier that drug companies spend far more on marketing (selling) their drugs than they do on research and development. I personally find that very scary! When you find the answers to these questions, let me know. I'm curious to see if you find what I found.

Honestly, is there money in finding a cure for AIDS,

cancer, lupus and many other major diseases? Treatment provides residual (recurring) income for drug companies and let's face it...doctors receive residual income too from the return of the patient. A cure could potentially cut off a future revenue stream (aka patient). As I said before, many conspiracy theorists believe that cures exist for most diseases, but that a cure isn't financially beneficial for those who benefit from treating symptoms. I would like to believe in the good of people, so I pray that no one could be evil enough that they would suppress the research and development that could be lead to a cure of any disease.

I've often wondered, 'What drug side effects aren't acceptable to doctors?' What side effects aren't acceptable to you? When you're prescribed a drug, do doctors even discuss the issue of side effects with you? My personal experience is that some do and many don't.

The primary contributors to medical drugs in our society are pharmaceutical companies, biotech companies and universities. Some drugs may be fast-tracked based on its need and other variables, but still the safety data is provided by the contributing companies or organizations themselves. These drug companies practically police themselves.

Like you, I wanted to know when humans began using all these unnatural, man-echomade drugs. I'm also curious to know who's right...Allopathic or Homeopathic doctors. I'm pretty sure that like Democrats and Republicans, these doctors need to meet somewhere in the middle for the good of Americans. The odds of that happening appear to be slim to none.

I recall discussing homeopathic options with KJ's allopathic doctors. It amazes me that despite the fact that their treatments weren't working, KJ's allopathic doctors wouldn't even listen to me or consult with a homeopathic doctor. Why are many allopathic doctors so closed minded about natural cures? Why were they insulted when I told them that I would rather have KJ take more Vitamin C over steroids? Could the hesitancy of a collaboration be over MONEY? Hey, I'm just asking. We all know that money is the root of all evil.

Allopathic doctors are taught little about natural cures in medical school. When I put KJ on a high dose of vitamin C, I noticed a significant difference in his health and his labs showed less lupus activity. Of course, doctors said that it was a coincidence and that his drugs were finally working. So many coincidences.

I understand that there's less money to be made with vitamin C than there is with the various drugs that supposedly boost the immune system. KJ is so sick of prednisone. Here's an important question for you. Did you know that there are no reported deaths from vitamins and minerals? At least I couldn't find any. If you find any of these reports, please let me know.

Ask most homeopathic doctors and they will tell you that they rarely receive referrals from their allopathic partners. I personally tried to get KJ's allopathic doctors to work with homeopathic doctors and the allopathic doctors refused. Most insurance plans won't even cover visits to homeopathic doctors. I know. I've been there. We had to pay cash for the visit, tests and treatments. As a matter of fact, when I had KJ's mercury fillings removed, I even had to pay cash for that. Removal of these horrible amalgams was considered cosmetic instead of medically necessary.

As a **SMART PATIENT**, you have to be prepared to ask questions. Not just about procedures and operations, but also about the drugs you're prescribed. Prescription drugs have a history of death. No-one can dispute this history. Drugs kill. Arm yourself with knowledge. Choose wisely!

Chapter 4

Your Checklist

Let's be clear, **THE DUMB PATIENT** isn't about doctor bashing. I do know some great doctors. KJ had a primary care doctor named Dr. Amber Denham of Baton Rouge. She was absolutely wonderful! We haven't had another Primary Care Physician (PCP) since. She would be that difficult to replace. KJ also had a Nephrologist, Dr. Melanie McKnight who would take the time to listen and discuss all of my concerns with me. I didn't say that she agreed with everything that I said, but she did listen. Another great doctor is a pediatric cardiologist, Dr. Brummand of Our Lady of the Lake. He was absolutely fantastic. I could genuinely see the pain and disappointment on his face when he heard some of the issues that KJ was having with other doctors. I would have loved to take all three of those doctors with us when we moved to Atlanta, but I checked my budget and it just wouldn't work.

The pediatric unit of Baton Rouge General, Bluebonnet helped me to realize that some hospitals actually do their job and they do it well. I must tell you that I'm not a fan of their emergency room (my opinion is that they were really slow and disorganized), but I do recommend the hospital as a whole and unless you get a direct admit, you have to go through the emergency room to get there. I also highly recommend nurse practitioners. Nurse practitioners have the compassion of nurses combined with the knowledge of medical doctors. I love them.

I know you chose to read this guide because you're tired of being a **DUMB PATIENT** and you're not ready to cross over to the controversial and disrespected world of being a **SMART PATIENT!** You've waited patiently, so here's your basic checklist. I'm going to keep it simple stupid (kiss) because when we face a medical crisis, the last thing that I want you to have to do is to remember a long list that of recommendations that I've given you. Yes, my friend, I will cover each point in detail for you in the following chapters! Your checklist is:

1.   *Know your rights!*

2.   *Be prepared!*

3.   *Get or become an advocate!*

4.   *Be proactive!*

As you can see, this checklist is purely based on common sense (another book). As you have also learned, when it comes to doctors we tend to throw common sense out of the window because we're too busy trusting them with our lives. I'm pretty sure that most of you are aware of the fact that you should already be doing most of the things on this checklist. It just seems that when speaking with a doctor, a lot people just feel intimidated!

Why the intimidation? I guess it's similar to discussing building a car with a car engineer. Engineering is his/her specialty and a novice would justifiably (kind of) believe that there's no way s/he could teach this trained engineer something that they don't already know. Is this thinking logical? Absolutely not, but it's understood. So let's delve right into your checklist.

Chapter 5

Know Your Rights

1. *You have the right to remain silent.*

2. *You have the right to an attorney.*

3. *Anything you say can and will be used against you in a court of law.*

Ok. I can see that I brought back memories for a few of you. Naughty. Naughty. Maybe one of your 'what happens in Vegas' moments didn't work out so well. I hope I made you smile for just a minute. Now let's get serious.

When you visit your doctor's office, have you ever felt like a criminal when you tried to make them honor your rights as a patient? Some doctors can make you feel that if you just come to the doctor's appointment and keep your mouth shut, that everything will be just fine.

I'm sure most doctors don't intentionally try to make us feel as if we're beneath them; however, we tend to get that uncomfortable feeling with many doctors from time to time. I can honestly say that many doctors have tried to make me feel very uncomfortable. More than a handful of doctors have attempted to belittle me and make me feel as if I'm a subordinate. It didn't work. I still forged ahead.

Question. Do you know what informed consent is? As a new patient to a physician's office, you sign a form that explains your medical rights. Do you trust doctors so much, that you don't even read the forms to know exactly what you're signing? Do you know your rights? Do you know what HIPAA (Health Insurance Portability and Accountability Act of 1996)? If a hospital or medical practice is doing their job, you should sign a HIPAA form for every office or hospital. Do you even understand what you're signing? HIPAA is a book within a book, so please research HIPAA. It's not realistic for us to discuss it here in its entirety, but we can do so on The Dumb Patient blog.

When you begin a relationship (doctor/patient relationship) with a new doctor, before we even sit down with him/her, you're given a stack of papers to 'read' and sign. Some of these papers pertain to your rights as a patient. They're often referred to as the Patient's Bill of Rights. You may be confused as to why I would chose 'KNOW YOUR RIGHTS' as the first and most important item on your checklist. My reasoning is very simple. At the end of the day, if you don't know what your rights are, then how can you ever demand the great healthcare that you want and deserve?

Let me digress for a minute. There are many people who would say that healthcare in America is a privilege, not a right. They say that great healthcare is given to those who can afford it. **THE DUMB PATIENT** is not here to debate our screwed up healthcare system. It's realistic to believe that those who don't have access to healthcare will be less likely to read this guide.

As you can recall, earlier in this chapter, I made a joke, regarding the rights of someone who has been arrested. Thanks to all the televised crime dramas, we have heard these rights repeated so many times, that most Americans can recite them by heart. We don't even need to go to law school or police training to repeat them without error.

Now I want you to imagine that you're pulled over by an overly aggressive police officer who insisted that you do things that went against your civil rights. This police officer insisted that you tell him where you got that pound of marijuana he found under your front seat of your car. Before you get all defensive, this is merely a hypothetical situation. We're role-playing. I already know that none of my readers would ever smoke weed or better yet, get caught with a pound of weed in their vehicle. Wink. Wink.

Anyway, a couple of things happened here:

1. *The police officer searched your vehicle. Did he or did he not violate your rights? Do you know?*

2. *He asked you to incriminate yourself. Did he or did he not violate your civil rights? Do you know?*

3. Did he even read you your rights prior
to asking you where you got that pound
of weed? Does he have to read them
before the search or after the search?
Do you know?

Here's another example referencing the practice of medicine. Let's say that your doctor prescribed a drug to help you with a medical problem that your child is having. As a parent, you've never heard of the medication so you have some concerns and some very specific and logical questions. You also want to discuss another drug that you learned of. This drug treats the same complications. That's a reasonable request right?

Your baby girl's doctor hesitates to answer your questions. S/he doesn't even dispel your concerns, yet s/he doesn't address them either. The doctor also goes on to dismiss your questions regarding other medication options by merely saying that he has always *'preferred to use this drug'*, but s/he doesn't say why.

The doctor *'prefers to use this drug'*. I can't even begin to tell you how many times I heard that one. Well, what exactly does that mean? Does this drug work better or have fewer side effects? Has the drug been around longer? As a patient, you have the right to know what medication options are available to treat your illness or disease. You also have the right to know the drug's side effects, effectiveness and their contraindications. If a doctor refuses to have this conversation with you, s/he is

80

violating your rights.

What exactly are your rights as a patient? According to the Association of American Doctors and Surgeons in 1995, your Patient's Bill of Rights is as follows:

[1]All patients should be guaranteed the following freedoms:

- *To seek consultation with the doctor(s) of their choice;*
- *To contract with their doctor(s) on mutually agreeable terms;*
- *To be treated confidentially, with access to their records limited to those involved in their care or designated by the patient;*
- *To use their own resources to purchase the care of their choice;*
- *To refuse medical treatment even if it is recommended by their doctor(s);*
- *To be informed about their medical condition, the risks and benefits of treatment and appropriate alternatives;*
- *To refuse third-party interference in their medical care, and to be confident that their actions in seeking or declining medical care will not result in third-party-imposed penalties for patients or doctors;*

---

[1] Association of American Physicians and Surgeons

- *To receive full disclosure of their insurance plan in plain language, including:*

1. *CONTRACTS: A copy of the contract between the doctor and health care plan, and between the patient or employer and the plan;*

2. *INCENTIVES: Whether participating doctors are offered financial incentives to reduce treatment or ration care;*

3. *COST: The full cost of the plan, including copayments, coinsurance, and deductibles;*

4. *COVERAGE: Benefits covered and excluded, including availability and location of 24-hour emergency care;*

5. *QUALIFICATIONS: A roster and qualifications of participating doctors;*

6. *APPROVAL PROCEDURES: Authorization procedures for services, whether doctors need approval of a committee or any other individual, and who decides what is medically necessary;*

7. *REFERRALS: Procedures for consulting a specialist, and who must authorize the referral;*

8. *APPEALS: Grievance procedures for claim or treatment denials;*

9. *GAG RULE: Whether doctors are subject to a gag rule, preventing criticism of the plan.*

Here's another tidbit. In order for your doctor to accept your insurance plan, s/he may have agreed to give you additional rights as a patient. If you have any concerns whether your patient rights are being violated, a great place to start would be your insurance company. They can be your friend or your foe. That's another book.

Know your rights and make sure that your doctor does their part to honor them. Remember that you're the client and whether you have private insurance, Medicare or Medicaid, your doctor isn't working for free. You must demand the fair and ethical treatment that they are getting paid for. With some doctors, you must demand that they honor your rights.

Learn and understand informed consent. This is critical. Whether it's a drug, surgery or treatment options, you're entitled to all the information necessary to assist you in making a logical and reasonable decision. Informed consent. I can't stress this enough. Stand up and fight for your rights. If you can't or won't, find someone who will.

Chapter 6

Be Prepared

I want to begin this chapter by reminding you that doctors are only human and that humans can be extremely judgmental. I can understand why you would be confused with that statement. You want to know; 'What does judgmental have to do with being prepared'? Let me explain what I mean with an example.

Recently, I was going from Atlanta to Savannah to join my better half, Dr. Estrada, Ph.D., for a nuclear medicine conference that he was attending. Since Atlanta to Savannah was only a 4.5 hour bus ride, I decided to dare the exciting Greyhound experience. Besides, it was just too tedious and expensive to fly such a short distance and driving made little sense. Ken (Dr. Estrada) had driven his truck and we didn't need to have two vehicles in Savannah.

While I was standing in the Greyhound line to check my one bag, I noticed an upset young lady who was accompanied by her young son. She bypassed the line and went directly to the ticket counter. Yep, I was next and she took my spot. Ultimately, she had gone back to the ticket agent who had just assisted her in purchasing a ticket. I could hear this young lady discussing that she had made reservations online to purchase tickets for 1 adult and 1 child.

Here's the problem. When the customer initially went to the ticket agent and showed the agent the printed paper with the reservation she had made online, the ticket agent only charged her for one adult full price ticket. The Greyhound ticket agent did not give the young lady a ticket for a child. No biggie right? WRONG! If you're unfamiliar with the policies of Greyhound, you wouldn't think that leaving out a child's ticket is a big deal. However, in fact, it's a huge issue. Let me tell you why something that seems so simple is in fact a serious error.

See, when you purchase an adult ticket you can also buy a child's ticket at a discounted price. When you go to purchase a ticket for a child by itself, you are charged a full price adult ticket. Depending on where you're travelling to, the difference been a discounted child ticket and a full price adult ticket could be hundreds of dollars. This young lady and her son were going from Atlanta to Michigan. That's a good distance and the price to purchase an adult ticket for her child was about $150. This upset and stranded mom didn't have an extra $150.

Unfortunately, the appearance of the young lady perpetuated the stereotype of a low income, minority and single mom. She wore a rag on her head and her and her child's clothing wasn't very neat. To add insult to injury, the young lady wasn't very articulate either. Thus, the employees at this Greyhound treated her with very little respect. It was as if she was unimportant to their company. The ticket agent rudely dismissed her and told her that she didn't know her son was with her and it wasn't her job to read the whole reservation that the young lady presented to her. Again, this mom didn't have the extra money and she was going to be stranded at the Atlanta Greyhound Station.

So, of course I had to step in. I personally can't stand bullies and I truly felt like the Greyhound agent was bullying this young mom! Now, keep in mind that I'm also a customer of Greyhound and I'm seeking the same low cost mode of travel as the young lady who was having complications. I believe the difference in the eyes of the employees was that I was well dressed in a 2 piece casual pants suit, blouse, high heeled shoes, jewelry and my hair was looking absolutely fierce (as Tyra Banks would say)! Wouldn't you know it, when I stepped in, the employees' tones and demeanors with me was completely different than the tones they used with the other young lady!

You see, the Greyhound staff members viewed me as an articulate, intelligent, professional business woman who merely *chose* to use their bus service. This belief was evident in the way that the Greyhound staff treated me. They viewed me as a valuable commodity and they showed me that they didn't want to lose my future business. Their first impression of me is why I believe that Greyhound was willing to work with me in order to resolve this mom's issue. On the contrary, Greyhound's perception of this young lady was that she was poor and had no other option but to use Greyhound because it was cheap. In my opinion, the staff at that Greyhound believed that she needed them more than they needed her. They didn't seem to value her business much.

Remember, I wanted to use Greyhound's services for the exact same reason that this young lady did. IT WAS CHEAP! However, I was more prepared to be received in a professional manner than this mom was. Does appearance really make that much of a difference in how you're treated? Unfortunately, it does. Most people form their first impression of you based upon what they see. First impressions are lasting impressions and they're difficult to overcome. After going back and forth with the staff, Greyhound issued her a voucher for the difference in fares and the mom and her son was on the next bus to Detroit.

Are you wondering what the Greyhound story has to do with you being prepared when you visit your doctor? Again, it's sad to admit it, but the first part of being prepared is to go to your doctor's appointment dressed in a manner that will force them to take you seriously. If you go there looking like a clown (pun intended), you better be prepared to juggle. If you go to your appointment looking like a bum (pun intended), you had better be prepared to beg exceptionally hard to get the respect, and quality healthcare you need. I know it's sad, but in most cases, it's true. In all cases, doctors are human.

Now, don't get carried away. You don't have to arrive to your doctor's appointment dressed in your

Sunday's best or the finest couture, but you do need to be clean and tidy. Don't try to fight this system. I know what I'm talking about. I've seen the looks that others have received from simply being improperly dressed. Yes, there may have been other factors involved, but I'm pretty sure that attire also played an initial role.

I don't want to sugarcoat things for you. Your clothing can stand in the way of you receiving quality healthcare. It may sound harsh, but I'm truly telling you this for your own good. I sincerely have your best interest at heart. So, go ahead and drop the ego and swallow your pride. You know whether you've gone to the doctor improperly dressed or not. If this applies to you, fix it immediately.

I'm not going to draw a diagram to show you what to wear. You must be willing to use common sense when it comes to your attire. For example: If you work in the construction industry (or something similar) and you're going to see your doctor straight from work, or on your lunch break; then more than likely, you're going to be a bit tad dirty. Again, make sure you're just dirty and not funky! There's a huge difference between funky and dirty. If you're going to visit your doctor directly from a messy job, then it's reasonable for you to be unkempt. However, if you have the time and opportunity to get cleaned up a little before your appointment, you should absolutely do so.

Are you still trying to put it all together? It's very simple. I don't want your clothes to be a distraction to your doctor and their office staff. You may already have other stereotypes and hurdles to overcome. Let's not add another one that isn't necessary.

What are the other hurdles? Let me break it down even further. When visiting doctors, men are typically treated better than women. Why? There are a few reasons why I believe this happens. Most doctors are men and men tend to render more respect to other men. Keep in mind that women are usually perceived as emotional and illogical creatures. Women tend to speak of their instincts (I did at first); whereas men tend to state their concerns as if it's a known fact and no room for wavering. Hey, it's well documented that men and women simply have different communication styles. The way women communicate can work against us when talking with our doctors.

When visiting doctors...age also matters! Yep. Physicians can be ageists. The concerns of young men, women and the elderly are often given less weight than the concerns of people (primarily men) in their 40's and early 50's. Why is that? Many doctors believe that the young are too immature to understand their own needs. Unfortunately, the elderly tend to get it both ways. They're often treated as if their old or as if they're still a child.

Race does matter. In America, we often like to pretend that racism doesn't exist anymore. In reality, it's alive, well and vibrant in many communities. There are still towns where the races live on opposite sides of the railroad tracks. I don't feel the need to elaborate on this racism in **THE DUMB PATIENT**. If you choose to live in a bubble by thinking that all is fair, just and equal in America, then live well my friend. I'm not here to bust your bubble. I will say that I have done business as T. M. Phenezy since 1998 because to be perceived as a white man (obviously, this is before they meet me) has been beneficial to my career and opened many doors.

Far too many patients also have to overcome educational and economic stereotypes. Let's face the facts. If you're considered uneducated, inarticulate or poor, there are doctors who would choose to believe that you just can't understand their complex practice of medicine. It's also a misconception that poor people aren't educated. There are a lot of poor people with professional degrees. In every economy, you can find a lot of unemployed college graduates.

When I initially began to negotiate the medical system in 2007, I had 3 main barriers to overcome.

1. *Perceived youth (I look darn good for my age).*

2. *I'm a woman.*

3. *I'm a minority.*

Why did I begin to navigate the medical system in 2007 when KJ didn't get ill until 2008? That was no misprint. My first battle with the medical system was when I was extremely ill. If I have time, I may share a tad bit more in respect to my personal illness in the final chapter, if not, we can chat about it on **THE DUMB PATIENT** blog. Hang in there. Curiosity is great for you.

As I was saying...When KJ and I walked into a doctor's office, the staff saw what they perceived to be just another young, Black single mom. As I revealed to you earlier in your guide, before I put my foot down and demanded respect, I was dismissed as if I was irrelevant. I felt like a mere dollar ($) sign to doctors. Has a business ever made you feel like they only wanted your money? Did you want to continue to do business with them? From personal experience, I can tell you that when a business or doctor doesn't value me as a client, it doesn't feel good. It especially sucks when you're made to feel unimportant in doctor/patient relationship.

When I finally got tired of the bullshit (no pun intended), I decided to show some Marine Corps spirit and pride. I demanded respect. I was then labeled as being an aggressive, belligerent and angry Black woman. You should know that the adjectives aggressive and angry are common stereotypes placed upon Black women in America. These stereotypes are especially used against single Black women.

To make matters worse, because I was a young (perceived not reality), single mom, many of KJ's doctors automatically assumed that I was also poor. I find that thought extremely funny and insulting. I was surely poor as a Marine, but not anymore. How little did these doctors actually know about me? Very little.

To tie this chapter together, just imagine if I had also walked into the doctor's office with my hair in disarray and KJ's and my clothing were dirty and in shambles. What type of reception would I have received from them? The thought of this type of ignorance is so scary to me that I don't want to visualize it. I don't even want to discuss that possibility because the mere idea of the added stereotype due to my clothing chills and disturbs me. I don't want to fathom the direction that this book would have taken if I would not have taken pride in our clothing and appearance. If I had taken that approach, I honestly don't believe that there would be a KJ today or a book of this nature to even write.

So, you and I just spent a long time confabulating (I just wanted to use a SAT word) over your appearance for your doctor visit. You must understand that I really need you to make a great first impression when you walk into a doctor's office. As I said earlier, a first impression is a lasting impression and a lasting impression is difficult to change. Choose wisely when dressing for your appointment.

Being prepared doesn't stop with your appearance. The next step in being prepared is to have a general idea regarding what's going on with the health of you or your loved one. I'm not saying that you should go to the doctor with your own diagnosis. I'm referring to the fact that you should be aware of your symptoms (if any). If you feel fine, be able to communicate that fact. If your appointment is for a basic physical, then this part may or may not apply to you AT THAT PARTICULAR TIME, but this information will be useful in the future!

When a **SMART PATIENT** has an ailment, you must be able to successfully explain your symptoms to your doctor. Please don't make your doctor guess how you feel. It's unfair and unrealistic to expect a doctor to know your body. That's your responsibility not your doctor's.

Preparation for your appointment can start at home or your office. Before you go to your doctor's visit, write down your symptoms and questions on a sheet a paper. When you do this in advance you'll find yourself thinking clearly at the doctor's office and you'll be under less pressure to recall your earlier thoughts. Having your thoughts on paper is especially critical if you end up with one of those 7 minute doctors that we discussed earlier in this guide.

Again, I have to trust you to use common sense. If you're on your way to the emergency room, please don't pull over to the side of the road to write down your symptoms and questions and then blame it on "The **DUMB PATIENT**". Please just go straight to the emergency room. Geez (rolling my eyes). However, if you have a scheduled doctor's appointment, take a few minutes to jot down your symptoms and any questions you may have for your doctor or billing.

If you're not a verbal communicator, writing your thoughts on paper is your perfect solution. Even the worst doctor should want to receive some sort of feedback from his/her patient. Tell your doctor that you wrote a list of your symptoms and the questions you have and then hand him/her your *LEGIBLE* notes to review.

As you recall when discussing your rights as a patient in Chapter IV, your doctor has to address your concerns in one way or the other. If they can't address your concerns, then s/he should refer you to someone who can. If s/he won't do either, then I would find another doctor, quickly. Don't forget to file a complaint if you deem it necessary.

Let me explain the importance of clear communication to you. In 2010, my father, Alton Anderson, went to a metro Detroit emergency room for stomach pain. Ultimately, this hospital admitted him and began to treat my father for chest pain. I wish I could tell you that this is a joke! This incident really did happen to my father.

During the time that my dad (Alton) was in the hospital, KJ, my mom and I were residing in Baton Rouge, La. We had moved there to be closer to family, so KJ was receiving the bulk of his medical care at Our Lady of the Lake in Baton Rouge. Coincidentally, at the time (2010) that my father was having this 'chest pain' (remember that it was really stomach pain), I was also writing a business plan to start a patient advocacy company called National Patient Advocate Institute (NPAI).

In dismay, my father called me on the phone from across the country. He was extremely angry, upset and frustrated because the doctors at the hospital weren't listening to him. These doctors were literally telling Alton that he had come to the hospital complaining of chest pain while simultaneously running tests on his heart.

I have to tell you that although my father is in his early 60's, he still has all the good sense that GOD had given him. He told me that he had never, ever complained of chest pains to anyone at the hospital. To make matters even worst, the doctors still weren't treating or acknowledging the issues he had with his stomach. My father's tummy was still hurting! This is so unfunny that you can't help but to laugh. My father had two obstacles to overcome.

1. *He's a senior citizen.*

2. *He's an ethnic minority.*

Due to all of the discomforting on the job training that I received from dealing with KJ's illness (and mine too), I was truly prepared to go to battle and win the war for my father. By this time, I had learned plenty of medical terminology. I understood blood tests and lab results without even looking at them. I knew (still do) how to read EKG's, echo cardiograms and many other tests. There was no need for the doctors to 'dumb it down' for me. I was no longer a **DUMB PATIENT**! I could speak the language of physicians. The fact that I was forced to learn this information to fight for great healthcare for my son is scary and sad, isn't it?

Please allow me to brag. It took me less than one day to rectify the issue with my father. On the phone, from across the country, I was able to get the hospital doctors and staff back on track. After my conversation with my father's doctor, the physician thought that I was in the medical field. The doctor asked my father whether or not I was a nurse. They didn't believe that I was a doctor because I didn't introduce myself as Doctor So & So.

Here's another so unfunny for you. By the time I finished talking with my father's doctor; this doctor was confused as to why the hospital was ever focusing on my dad's chest. There was no positive EKG, echo walkcardiogram or chest x-ray. Someone had said that my father complained about having chest pain and everyone ran with it, despite the fact that he kept telling them otherwise.

By the end of the day, the hospital did treat my father's stomach pain. If my memory serves me correctly, they kept him in the hospital for another day for observation and then discharged him to follow-up with the outpatient plan that his doctor and I had worked out.

As I stated at the beginning of this chapter, doctors are human. Humans are judgmental. We, as patients, must eliminate as much of human error and judgment as possible by simply showing up to do business the right way. Just remember to **BE PREPARED!** It's your choice. Choose wisely!

Chapter 7

Get or Become Your Own Advocate

The Freedictionary.com defines an advocate as '*One that argues for a cause; a supporter or defender.*'

I remember the first time that KJ told me that my picture will be on the walls of every doctor's office in the country with a sign that says, 'Don't let this woman in!' Some people would be offended by that statement. Not me. I was encouraged. I was proud! Why? His statement told me that KJ knows that I will fight for him 'By any means necessary'. KJ is absolutely right.

If you're sensitive, you may want to skip the next few paragraphs. Matter of fact, this entire chapter will be very blunt and may contain some strong language (profanity). It's now time for you to do some self-reflection and to make some difficult decisions. If you avoid making decisions, go ahead and skip to the final chapter (yep the next chapter requires self-reflection too) and let's pray that you've already acquired enough information that you will be successful with the healthcare of you or a loved one moving forward. Maybe good healthcare is good enough for you. Keep in mind that good is the enemy of great.

What is an advocate? Simply put, it's someone who will go to war for you and yours when the **SHIT** hits the fan. Your life may depend on the ability of your advocate to communicate and fight for your needs effectively. S/he must do so articulately and without pause.

Here's a quick example. Recently, the father of my cousin-in-law, Kim Jones, had to undergo surgery for gangrene. She described how the doctors told her family that they had to cut off one toe to remove the gangrene from his feet. After her father was recovering in his hospital room, the doctors said they had to take him back to surgery to remove another toe. This cycle repeated one more time to remove a third toe. According to Kim, this hospital put her father under anesthesia 3 times in approximately 36 hours. Her siblings were concerned because their father was unresponsive. Of course he's unresponsive. He's high on pharmaceutical drugs!

To know Kim is to love her or hate her. I love her because she's extremely direct and you know exactly where you stand with her. She loves me! Smile. Kim is also very articulate and smart, but, when she gets angry...watch out! I had to explain to Kim, that when dealing with the hospital, doctors and their staff, she must control her emotions and anger or they will only see her and hear her as a ghetto rat (A girl or guy who hangs out in all the ghetto bars and clubs...urban dictionary). Kim is ready to go to war for her father, but she needed that one bit of information in order to do so properly. Armed with the right attitude and the right information, Kim was ready to properly advocate for her father. Unfortunately, her father passed away soon after. RIP.

Like Kim, an advocate is not afraid to enter unfriendly territory. An advocate is like a bad ass, United States Marine who when ambushed with enemy fire, s/he will stand up with his flak jacket secure, firing back with his/her M-50 saying, 'Is that all you got mother fucka?' Yep, I said it. That's why Marines are the few and the proud. We not only go to war for our country, we'll win the battle too.

Ok, maybe that example may seem a bit extreme because doctors aren't our enemies. Most doctors have great intentions. I truly believe that if physicians understood that medical errors would decrease significantly with patient involvement, doctors would be more on board with this idea. We should probably tell them that the fewer medical errors they make, the lower their malpractice insurance will be. How's that for an incentive? Money!

I do want you to ask a few people in your life who have had a serious healthcare problem, whether or not they feel like they're kept in the dark by their doctor regarding their healthcare decisions and choices. I sometimes compare it to the military's don't ask, don't tell policy. If you don't ask any questions, they won't tell you anything except what to do and what drugs to take. Raise your hand if you want this type of relationship with your doctor? Do you?

Let's face it. The practice of medicine is extremely

difficult. Most people consider it an imperfect science. Many people consider it more of an art. So, your advocate must have thick skin. If you're the advocate, you must have thick skin. If you're a woman or a minority, your skin must be exceptionally thick.

It's also important for you to know that an advocate may not always be correct when advocating. Therefore, your advocate must also be willing to compromise and negotiate for reasonable and logical outcomes. Navigating the medical system for someone you love is extremely frightening for the average Joe or Suzy, but someone, somewhere has to accomplish this mission on a daily basis. It's the reality of life. People get sick. What happens next is between you and GOD.

You may be surprised to know that I've even had doctors tell me crazy stories about when they were disrespected while seeking medical care outside of their specialty. Their fellow colleagues didn't even respect their medical degree. In my opinion, doctors who have had to navigate the medical system for themselves or a family member tend to be much more compassionate.

Nurse Practitioner Andrea Bossie of the Transplant Unit at Piedmont Hospital (great hospital) in Atlanta says that she rarely tells a doctor that she's a nurse practitioner. Why? She said that she doesn't tell them because many doctors won't respect her 20 years of experience as a nurse. How sad is that?

Doctors attend school for over 10 years and they still

don't know everything about the practice of medicine. They can't know everything. There are far too many specialties. Medicine and science is ever changing and every case is different. I can't count the number of times that a doctor told me how unique and complicated KJ's medical history was. The sad part is that these same doctors would note the differences regarding the course of his disease but still treat him based on how they've treated other patients with the same 'disease'. Their logic just didn't make any sense to me.

Again, this isn't a guide to bash doctors. It's a guide to increase your odds of receiving GREAT medical care. With GOD's grace, the great medical care that you receive will increase your lifespan. Some doctors and hospitals may be highly upset with this guide. Why? They will probably be upset because it will cause them to do some self-reflection. If they see a little of themselves in **THE DUMB PATIENT**, How to Avoid Death by Doctor, then they have the opportunity to make a change. If their medical practice has the 7 (approximate) minute rule then, they can fix it. If the doctor who gets upset with this guide is the type of doctor who avoids answering questions, then maybe s/he can begin to be more communicative and receptive to their patient's needs. Maybe that doctor is willing to see things from the eyes of a patient.

As a patient, you're probably reading this guide because you're tired of being a **DUMB PATIENT**. Do you really want to know, 'How to Avoid Death by

Doctor?' Well, you must get or become your own patient advocate. Yes, YOU! You have to begin by educating yourself. If you're afraid to tackle the system or you find the information too complex or confusing to retain, ask a family member or friend to help you or you can use an independent patient.

Many hospitals have some kind of patient advocate on staff. Their job is to ensure that the patient receives the best care possible. This advocate usually is an employee of the hospital. Using an advocate who's an employee of the hospital may or may not be a conflict. You must decide whether you believe a conflict of interest exists. In reality, this advocate's job, income and retirement are dependent upon keeping their position with the hospital. However, any advocate may be better than no advocate at all. Just pray that s/he has a conscience.

What does all of this mean to you? Allow me to play devil's advocate (pun intended) for a few minutes. Imagine that you're a patient in the hospital and you have found that a serious error has been committed. After speaking with the charge nurse and doctors assigned to your care, you continue to get the run around. I can practically guarantee that this scenario happens on a daily basis in one hospital or another.

So, seeking immediate help for your situation, you begin to reach out to the hospital's administrative staff. Alas, a patient advocate shows up at your beside. Yes! Thank you Jesus! Here's someone who's finally going to give you the assistance that you need. Suddenly you pause to think…a patient advocate?   This person is working 'only' on my behalf, right?

Honestly, it's difficult to say.   My personal experience with patient advocates who work for the hospital has shown me that there is conflict of interest. I recall discussing a problem with the hospital's advocate assigned to me and he refused to acknowledge the problem even though it was clear as day. I felt like I was in the middle of a tug and war. Even worst, I received the same political, babble BS (bullshit) that I had already heard. You know the words, 'Let me see what I can do.' This advocate refused to admit that the hospital was wrong or liable when they gave KJ a potassium IV. He just repeated over and over again that he would see what he could do. Do you know what he did? Nothing! He did nothing that I could quantify or qualify. I personally had to dig deeper into my foxhole and prepare for a long drawn out war.

Let me give you an analogy regarding conflict of interest that you can relate to.   Coastal southern California is without debate, extremely beautiful.   It offers you near perfect weather with beautiful mountain and ocean views. You can easily be in a swimming suit on the beach and a few hours later, you could be charging down the slopes of a mountain on your snow skis. Due to these luxuries, southern California is also extremely expensive.

When I was heavily invested in real estate, I owned a beautiful, million dollar condo (during those market conditions) in the M2i building in downtown San Diego. This unit occupied 2 stories and was the largest condo in the building. The M2i building is conveniently located 2 blocks from the San Diego Padres baseball stadium so it was the perfect location for someone who loved the fast pace of the downtown nightlife.

When I acquired the condo, it didn't have any occupants so I decided that I would find tenants to rent it for 6 months until I put it on the market to sell. I allowed a real estate agent to convince me that she could find a better, more qualified tenant for me in a timely manner. In the State of California, real estate agents could (I believe they still can) represent the buyer and the seller or the tenant and the landlord. When a real estate agent represents both parties, their job is to get the best deal for both sides. Often the two parties don't even speak with each other except through the agent. When a real estate agent represents both parties, they get to keep all of the commission. Good for them, right?!

To my surprise, about a week later, the agent called me on the phone to set up an appointment for me to review an application from a wonderful couple. Upon reviewing the application, I was impressed. They were employed-check! Great credit score-check! Outstanding references-check! Awww shucks. This couple only wanted to commit to a one year rental because they didn't want to pack up and move again in such a short span. I could understand that. Moving is so expensive. The problem: I only wanted to do a 6 month term so I could

105

sell the condo later. Darn it.

Most of the time, having a great tenant who's committed to staying in your property for one year is a great thing. However, to a real estate investor who's looking to sell quickly, having a long-term tenant could be a problem. However, because this was a well-qualified applicant, I agreed to the one year term, but I insisted on a clause that would allow me to pay their moving expenses if I sold the unit after 6 months of occupancy.

Looks like my real estate agent did a great job. She was truly working for me as my real estate advocate, right? Wrong! Wrong! Wrong! A few days after signing the lease, I met my new and extremely excited tenants at the property for the initial walk through. The unit's walls were freshly painted and the carpets had been cleaned. During the walk through, one of them stated that they wish that I would have considered a 6 month lease because they really wanted to buy a house around that time.

STOP THE PRESSES! Did my new tenants just tell me that they really only wanted a 6 month lease? How could this have gone wrong? Where did the miscommunication happen?

You know what went wrong? We both trusted someone to be our advocate who had a conflict of interest. Our real estate agent ultimately was only working for her pocketbook! She wasn't working for either of us. It's difficult to compete with her commissions. Ultimately, the tenants and I changed the rental agreement. I wanted to get some of my money back, but of course I couldn't get in touch with the agent to get a refund in the commission difference. Go figure, right?

Healthcare and real estate are not the only area in our lives where we depend on someone to advocate for us. We elect politicians to speak on our behalf, but sometimes, their actions are about self-preservation and lining their wallets (I'm still wearing my flak jacket). We also hire attorneys, retirement specialists and other professionals as advocates. We expect them to go to war on our behalf and fight for our needs. We expect them to sell us the best product, not the product that earns them most commission. We always want our advocates to be ethical, reliable and honest.

Look, most advocates are ethical and take pride in the jobs they perform for their clients. Just like any job, some advocates may carry the title while lacking the enthusiasm, ethical behavior and job performance. If you're seeking an advocate you must choose carefully.

When I was writing this chapter, I asked my mom if she would ever use a patient advocate who was employed by the hospital she was a patient of. My mom quickly and bluntly replied, 'I didn't know that hospitals had patient advocates!'

Wow. My mom had a great point. I then began to

reflect on how I learned about patient advocates. I remember calling an old client who's also a physician. I told him that I was having problems getting the right treatment for KJ and I didn't know who to speak with in the hospital. He told me that he couldn't remember the title (he's in private practice), but it would be someone in administration. So, I decided to Google it. Yep, I'm a Google scholar! That's an inside joke.

Like me and my mom, if you aren't aware of the hospital's patient advocates, then you surely don't know that you should ask for him/her. My curious mind wanted to know how many people knew that some hospitals have a patient advocate. There's only one way to find out quickly; I began to make calls to friends and family who weren't in the medical industry.

To avoid conflict, my question was simple and direct. 'Did you know that some hospitals have patient advocates?' Most of the people I called had zero knowledge of them. I did speak with a couple of people who had heard of them. So, we discussed their experience in detail to see if it differed from mine.

Martin and Tina Harkless is a beautiful couple who have been married for 25 years. Martin and I served in the Marine Corps together when I was younger. He was always old (joke)! Mr. & Mrs. Harkless learned about patient advocates when their son was in the hospital several years ago. They spoke highly of the lady who was their hospital assigned advocate. What I found most interesting is that they felt that the assistance she rendered to them border lined career suicide for her. They also felt that she was only able to be so bold because, maybe, just maybe, she had information on a few doctors or on the hospital that protected her position. Interesting point of view, isn't it?

I also spoke with Delisa Lender. When her mom was on her death bed in the hospital, she was advised to seek the help of the hospital's patient advocate. Unfortunately, that conversation between Delisa and the advocate never happened. Delisa's mom passed away while she was in route to speak with the advocate. RIP. Delisa was disappointed and upset that no-one had told her about the advocate sooner. Everyone else that I spoke with was unaware that the advocacy position existed in a hospital.

Don't gamble with your health! You're extremely important to many people. Ultimately, if you're not getting the treatment that you need from your hospital or doctor's medical 'practice', you need to do one or more of the following:

1. *Educate yourself to become your own advocate.*

2. *Find a family member or friend who's willing and able to advocate for you.*

3. *Trust the advocate that the hospital assigns to you.*

4. *Hire an independent advocate who will work for you.*

Dr. Ken Estrada and I created the National Patient Advocate Institute (NPAI) for Americans who seek an independent patient advocate to assist them with navigating the maze called health care. At the NPAI, we don't administer diagnoses. We don't write prescriptions or refer you to doctors. What we will do is assist you in navigating the healthcare system. We will also go to bat for you when your insurance company denies a claim and it appears that there's no justifiable reason to deny it. If there's a legal claim against a hospital, doctor or clinic, we'll refer you to one of our affiliate attorneys to review your case.

The NPAI will go even further by fighting for fair and lawful treatment of patients, veterans and elderly with disabilities against schools, employers, and other organizations who discriminate against our members. Our services are fairly inexpensive for individuals, families and organizations. For those who need our services yet can't afford the membership cost, we seek out sponsorships from local businesses on your behalf.

There are many other patient advocate companies. Just Google away and you'll find a long list. They all function differently, but have the similar goals. As with anything, you must do your research to determine which company will best fit your needs. Don't forget to ensure that these companies aren't receiving monies from drug companies, hospitals and other organizations which may conflict with the assistance you will receive from them.

When I was doing my patient advocate research for **THE DUMB PATIENT**, I was able to find one common denominator. Everyone whom I spoke with said that if money was not an object, they would prefer to use an independent patient advocate versus the advocate provided by the hospital. Everyone wanted to eliminate the possibility of a conflict. Although NPAI has affiliations with doctors, nurses and other healthcare professionals to assist you, we would never assign an advocate to work on your case who has a current, known relationship with your provider in question. We carefully work to eliminate conflicts.

Unfortunately, I know better than most that when dealing with complex medical issues, emotions are extremely difficult to control. Sadly, I had to learn my advocacy skills while watching my one and only child suffer. I never in my wildest dreams thought that I would have to dedicate months of my time becoming a self-taught advocate in order to keep my one and only child alive. This process has been the most challenging and heart wrenching experience that I've ever had to endure. When you consider that I'm a U.S. Marine Corps Veteran who grew up in and on the streets of Detroit, it puts into perspective how difficult the walk with GOD and KJ was.

Trust me when I tell you that most people can't fathom that I was ever a Marine. First impressions can also be deceiving. When people first look at me, they see a very feminine woman in 6" stilettos (wink wink).

People who don't know me can't seem to imagine me hiking and completing a 22 mile hump (hike) in the hills of California with full gear weighing more than half of my weight! Well, I did! Ernestine Buscagan and I made this trip while many male Marines who were twice our size, dropped out of the hump and had to 'get in the truck'. We were the only women in our unit at the time so Ernestine and I stuck together like glue.

My point is simple. That 22 mile hike was a walk in the park compared to navigating this cruel medical system on behalf of my son. Yes, KJ had to do the hard work; he fought to stay alive when so many believed it was impossible. KJ is my motivation for writing **THE DUMB PATIENT**. Far too many times, I've sat in waiting room with many parents who didn't even understand the basics of their children's labs. It's not their fault. We were all brainwashed as a child to believe that doctors have all the right answers regarding our healthcare.

I'm truly committed to educating our nation. I'm committed to being your advocate one way or another. Some people will hate me, but when you're fighting for positive change…hate happens. My dear friend, in order for you to Avoid Death by Doctor, you must arm yourself with the basic tools that I've already described for you.

1. *Know your rights.*

2. *Be prepared*

3. *Get or become an advocate*

4. *Be proactive (next chapter)*

If you need assistance navigating the 'practice' of medicine or you just want to be proactive in case the need arises, don't hesitate another moment to give us at NPAI a call. We will welcome and appreciate your membership. We have assembled a strong team of professionals who are just as passionate about advocacy as I am. Give us a call at 855-411-4032.

Chapter 8

Be Proactive

Let's KISS (Keep It Simple Stupid) again! You can't blame doctors for all of your health problems. You also can't blame them every time something goes wrong in your healthcare. Sometimes, doctors can only work with what they're given. At the end of every day you must accept the ultimate responsibility for your health and the health of your child. You can significantly reduce your chances of having serious medical issues by just being proactive.

Ok. I know you're wondering how being proactive can assist you with your medical care. Let's define proactive.

The freedictionary.com defines proactive as: *'Acting in advance to deal with an expected difficulty; anticipatory.'*

Businessdictionary.com defines proactive as: *'Action and result oriented behavior, instead of the one that waits for things to happen and then tries to adjust (react) to them. Proactive behavior aims at identification and exploitation of opportunities and in taking preemptory action against potential problems and threats, whereas reactive behavior focuses on fighting a fire or solving a problem after it occurs.'*

It doesn't matter which definition you use, it all boils down to YOU taking control and being held responsible for YOU and your healthcare! How do you do that? AH! It's so simple. You can begin by eating right, exercising, drinking responsibly and saying no to drugs and irresponsible sexual behavior. You need to know what medications you're prescribed, their doses and why you're taking them. These are all the things that we know we should do but far too many of us are too lazy to do them on a consistent basis. I know that I personally need to exercise more.

You have to understand the United States healthcare industry is a multi-trillion dollar industry. You don't need to help them make money! Preventable obesity, diabetes, heart disease, sexual transmitted disease and high blood pressure are high contributors to the burden of medical costs for United States citizens. We currently have millions of uninsured or under insured people who visit emergency rooms with avoidable medical issues. Do you bear any responsibility for these costs? Self-reflect on that.

I really need you to remember that doctors are human too. Yes, I said it again. Part of being proactive is for you to do your due diligence. I personally know people (especially women) who would drive farther to visit their hair dresser or barber than they will drive for a doctor's appointment to a GREAT doctor.

Ladies, be honest, how many times have you asked

another lady for a referral to her beauty salon? Why did you feel the need to ask for that referral? The answer is simple. Her hair was looking absolutely fabulous and you wanted your hair to look fabulous too.

Now ask yourself, when you see someone who's in fantastic shape and excellent health, why don't you ever ask them their health secret and for a referral to their primary care doctor, gym or personal trainer. Most people wouldn't consider asking a relative, yet alone a complete stranger, for a referral to their primary care doctor. Ask yourself, how far are you willing to go to accept responsibility for your healthcare and/or the healthcare of your family?

Now, I will say, that when families are preparing to give birth to a new child, they usually get a referral to an ob/gyn and a pediatrician. That's a great start, but we have to keep it going beyond childbirth and pediatrics. We can't stop using common sense when we get older. Yep. I said it. Everything in **THE DUMB PATIENT** is all about common sense. Use it.

KISS. When you have guests in town and you want to take them to a great restaurant, you usually ask a friend to recommend a unique and quality place to dine. When you need a great doctor, ask a friend. Now, keep in mind that your friend may be a **DUMB PATIENT**, so we need to make sure that they're giving you a great referral. Here are a few questions to ask when requesting referrals:

116

1. *How long have you been going to this doctor?*

2. *Does the doctor explain the medication prescribed?*

3. *Does the doctor spend enough time with you or do you feel rushed when you go to an appointment?*

4. *Does the doctor answer all your questions? (Also find out if they ever ask their doctor any questions.*

I'm really depending on you to use your common sense and think. Sometimes things happen that are out of our control. When that happens, in the Marine Corps we were taught that you must adapt, improvise and overcome. Most of the things that go wrong (and right) are because of the choices you have made. There's not much more for me to say regarding being proactive. It's common sense!

Before going forward to the final chapter, I want you to take some time to do some honest, self-reflection. What do you need to do differently to improve your health? What can you do differently to participate in your healthcare? What responsibility do you bear? Are you prepared to be an advocate or do you need to find one? Do you have all the necessary information about the drugs you're taking? Choose wisely.

Chapter 9

The Smart Patient

Life is all about choices. Some people choose to be good while others make the choice to be great. I'm sure you've heard the phrase, *'Good is the enemy of great'*. Ask yourself this question: Is a good doctor, good enough for you?

I engaged in a discussion regarding hospital care with, Dr. Kenwyn Estrada, Ph.D. (my man) and he said, *'Excellence is not a requirement in the practice of medicine. Providers just need to meet the basic standard of care.'* He also pointed out the fact that Joint Commission on the Accreditation of Healthcare Organization (JCAHO) now combined with the Center for Medicare & Medicaid Services (CMS) only requires providers to meet the standard of care.

This premise is simple. Do you remember in Chapter 1, when KJ and I left California to receive medical care elsewhere? Everyone told me that I wound never receive chelation therapy for mercury fillings (amalgams) in a conventional hospital. They were sure that an allopathic doctor would never order the treatment. These people weren't trying to be negative; they simply understood that to receive this chelation therapy for amalgams was outside of the standard of care for hospitals. They were really trying to protect KJ by referring us to 'alternative' doctors who were comfortable treating these issues.

You should also know that one case, like KJ's, does not make this treatment the 'standard of care'. There must be a documented pattern that will and can be subject to scrutiny by other doctors and researchers. Yes, regarding KJ, there is a pattern for treatment of mercury poison due to amalgams, but this pattern exists within the community of 'alternative' doctors. Most allopathic doctors are not as open to viewing the data of their 'alternative' counterparts. To this day, KJ is the only person in America (that I can find) who has received chelation therapy for mercury poisoning due to Amalgams in a traditional hospital.

As I said before, many people often ask me if I sued the dentist. No is my answer. I didn't sue for a couple of reasons. The first being that KJ and I were too busy fighting for his life to deal with a law suit. Secondly, I would have had to be extremely involved in the lawsuit because I couldn't find a medical malpractice attorney who was knowledgeable enough regarding the mercury in amalgams. Last but not least, I couldn't find an attorney who was brazen enough to even take this type of case. It would have been an uphill lawsuit because amalgams are considered 'standard of care' by many in the field of dentistry.

As previously stated, I know that there will be many
119

people in the healthcare industry who will be highly upset with this guide. Why? If you're that person, I challenge you to find something to learn in **THE DUMB PATIENT** that will make your medical practice better. I'm not the only person in America who's had horrible experiences with physicians. I'm merely a mouthpiece for the millions of people who chose not to share their experience.

If you're a physician, administrator of a hospital or staff of a medical practice, you can immediately improve your service by respecting all clients. Are you running the 7 minute medical practice? Are you truly informed about the drugs you prescribe? Do you thoroughly answer your patient's questions? Do you welcome questions and patient involvement? Do you consider the instinct of a mom or dad?

Hopefully those of you in the healthcare industry will use this guide to make your medical practice or hospital better. A child experienced unnecessary suffering due to the egos and prides of many doctors. KJ's suffering started in 2008 and on September 1, 2012, he received the gift of life with a kidney transplant. Why did he need a new kidney? Doctor's error! Yes. KJ's kidney failed because a doctor refused to acknowledge the concerns of his advocate (me). His kidney never, ever should have failed. This event should not have happened. Point blank!

Between 2008 and 2013, KJ fought to keep hope,

faith and life. He fought fearlessly and he fought successfully. Now he's coaching basketball, playing basketball, preparing for college and working on a company of his own. KJ's Story is far too complex and detailed to put in this guide. The purpose of **THE DUMB PATIENT** is to help you navigate the medical system. I merely used parts of KJ's Story to explain our personal experiences. I know you would like to know more about KJ, so I do promise you that I will share KJ's Story in detail soon.

Now that you're graduating to a **SMART PATIENT**, you should have a basic understanding on navigating the medical system. Use the tools and checklist that I have outlined here and add more tools to fit your personal scenario. Always remember to integrate common sense into your decisions. Despite what many physicians will tell you, I insist that you use your instincts. You know you better than anyone else knows you. If your instincts are never correct, then follow the system. If something doesn't sound right, it probably isn't.

Don't wait until you have an emergency to start using what you've learned here. It's so hard to learn CPR while administering it to save a life. Consider this checklist your CPR to great healthcare. Today you can start making healthy eating, exercising and great healthcare a part of your lifestyle. Expect it and go get it. If you still need additional help you can give us a call at

NPAI **(www.THENPAI.org**) to see how we can play an integral role in your healthcare plan. I practice what I preached not it's your turn. Together, let's create a generation of **SMART PATIENTS**.

THE DUMB PATIENT, How to Avoid Death by Doctor is merely a roadmap to assist you in your journey. The rest is up to you, your doctor and of course, your GOD. Choose wisely!

Notes

Notes

Notes

Notes